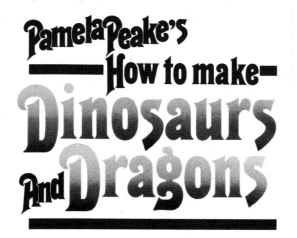

Collins Glasgow & London

First published 1976
Published by William Collins Sons and Company Limited
Glasgow and London

Photographs by Ian Atkinson
Copyright © Pamela Peake 1976
Printed in Great Britain
ISBN 0 00 411837 5
(cased)
ISBN 0 00 411839 1
(paperback)

Contents

The toys in this book are the copyright of the author,
Pamela Peake, and cannot be commercially manufactured
except under licence.

To my family

Also by Pamela Peake
Creative Soft Toy Making

Colour Illustrations

Notes

Useful addresses for toymaking equipment

The Needlewoman,
146–8 Regent Street,
London W1R 6BA

Fred Aldous Ltd,
P.O. Box 135,
37 Lever Street,
Manchester M60 1UX

Dryad,
Northgates,
Leicester

The above three companies supply a catalogue for a small fee.

John Lewis & Co. Ltd,
Oxford Street, London W1

Supplies fabrics, fur, felt, fillings and general toymaking equipment.

Ells and Farrier Ltd,
(The Bead House),
5 Princes Street,
Hanover Square,
London W1R 8PH

Supplies beads and sequins. Sample cards can be purchased for a small fee.

Metric measurements

Centimetres are given to the nearest 0·5 cm or half centimetre throughout the book. Since fabrics are now being sold by the metre, the equivalent 1 m = 1 yd has been used. Quantities under 1 m have been approximated to the nearest 5 cm.*

 Some retailers will cut only to the nearest 10 cm, so you may occasionally have to buy an extra 5 cm of fabric than the quantity actually required to make a toy.

1 Introducing Dinosaurs and Dragons

Belief in monsters has always been widespread, for there is hardly a country which does not contain a dragon, serpent, wyvern, cockatrice, basilisk or some such beast in its folklore or mythology. In many early European legends you find dragons living in caves guarding vast treasures of gold and jewels, or roaming the countryside capturing beautiful princesses and maidens. Consequently, tales of heroic deeds frequently depict young men slaying dragons and rescuing either the maidens or the gold.

In mediaeval paintings they are often used to represent evil, and no doubt this representation can be traced back to the Biblical snake in the Garden of Eden. There are many similarities between the use of snakes, serpents and dragons in this context. Christian legends are full of knights slaying dragons, such as St Michael and the Dragon of the Apocalypse or St George and the Dragon.

In contrast, the dragons of Chinese legends are always associated with benevolence and prosperity, frequently appearing as pleasant or happy individuals. The supreme being, the giant Pan Ku, created the universe with the help of four animals, one of these being a dragon. Every New Year, there is a festival to arouse the sleeping dragons so that they can produce rain for the forthcoming harvest. Fireworks were developed for this occasion, as they produced lots of noise. According to ancient Chinese writers, these dragons hatched as serpents but eventually, after thousands of years, grew into full-fledged dragons complete with horns and wings.

Many dragons and serpents have been recognized as relations of the reptiles – snakes and lizards – so it is not surprising that they were included in natural histories.

Such works were still being published as late as the eighteenth century. Although as exploration of the world progressed, the belief in dragons faded, by the time their actual existence ceased to be accepted they had become permanently incorporated into folk tales and fairy tales. Now, in the twentieth century, they are just as popular as ever, being found in stories of science fiction and literary tales.

The depths of the sea have been thought to contain their share of monsters, from giant octopuses to sea serpents, and it is these that have now taken the place of the dragons of old. Many lakes have their legends. There is the Loch Ness monster from Scotland, and the Manipogo from Lake Manitoba in Canada, to mention just two. There is no concrete evidence to prove their existence, but this does not stop people from believing in monsters, for we all seem to be compelled by a need for fantasy.

That fact is stranger than fiction was demonstrated about a hundred and fifty years ago, when some English scientists found various giant-size fossil bones. They thought that dragons could be discounted and they felt reluctant to accept any other popular explanation, namely that these were the bones of giants or of animals which had perished during the Great Flood of Biblical times. A Sussex doctor, Gideon Mantell, described a giant plant-eating reptile from some teeth and a few bones, while an Oxford University geologist, Dean Buckland, found bones which he identified as belonging to an enormous meat-eating reptile. The likes of these reptiles were difficult for scientists to accept, but it could not be doubted that at some time in the past giant reptiles had lived. We now know that these were the first discoveries of the Dinosaurs. This name was given to the giant reptiles by Richard Owen in 1841. It is a Greek word meaning 'terrible lizards'.

Owen was fascinated with the idea of prehistoric monsters, and also investigated the Dragon's teeth sold by apothecaries in China, which he identified as the fossil remains of mammals and even of ancient man. Owen commissioned Waterhouse Hawkins to build life-size models, which were eventually erected in Crystal Palace Gardens, London, where they can still be seen today.

During the 1870s, Professors Marsh and Cope were finding fossils in North America, and since this time many more have been found all over the world in every continent. Some skeletons are incomplete, but all the information has been used to piece together a picture of prehistoric times. It has been shown that dinosaurs varied greatly in size and shape: while many were large, some were about the size of domestic chickens. Other reptiles were found with the dinosaurs, some of them so well known that we can hardly think of the Age of Dinosaurs without them. These are the ichthyosaurs, plesiosaurs, pterosaurs and Dimetrodon. From the fossil remains, it soon became clear that the dinosaurs were in reality composed of two very different groups of reptiles. The first is identified by having bird-like hip bones and is called the Ornithischia. The second group has lizard-like hip bones and is called the Saurischia.

Ornithischia

ornithopods (bird-footed duck-bills and iguanodons)
stegosaurs (plated dinosaurs)
ankylosaurs (armoured dinosaurs)
ceratopsians (horned dinosaurs)
All the ornithischians were plant-eaters, that is, vegetarians.

Saurischia

sauropods (giant amphibious dinosaurs)
theropods (beast-footed carnivorous dinosaurs)

The meat-eaters or carnivores all lived on land, while the amphibious group were vegetarians, probably living on land and in water.

The history of the earth for which there is a good fossil record is divided into three major eras called the Palaeozoic (ancient life), the Mesozoic (middle life) and the Cenozoic (new life). The Age of Reptiles, and of dinosaurs in particular, occurred during the Mesozoic era, which lasted for about 160 million years. In many books written about these animals, the Mesozoic is further divided into the Triassic, Jurassic and the Cretaceous periods. Dinosaurs made their appearance 240 million years ago, during the Triassic, as did several other reptiles like the ichthyosaurs, plesiosaurs and Dimetrodon.

The Jurassic period began 200 million years ago and lasted for 65 million years. It was very warm and humid, with a luxurious vegetation of conifers, ferns, cycads and mosses. This period saw the dinosaurs as the rulers of the earth. There were the stegosaurs, ornithopods and the giant amphibious sauropods.

The Cretaceous period began 135 million years ago and lasted for 65 million years. It was more temperate than the Jurassic, with forests of the first flowering plants, and there were vast herds of vegetarian ornithischians preyed upon by the giant carnivores, which were at their zenith.

Towards the end of the Cretaceous all the dinosaurs and many of the other reptiles died out completely. This is a great puzzle and many suggestions have been put forward to account for it. The only reptiles which have survived through till today are the crocodiles, turtles, snakes and lizards, and the Tuatara from New Zealand.

So, while we have the fantasy of modern unknown monsters supposedly lurking in the oceanic depths or in space, we also have the reality of dinosaurs. Generations of children grow up, thirsting for information about them. They are featured in Natural History books, as exhibits in museums, in dinosaur reconstruction gardens, and their popularity is exploited in stories, films, television and comic strips. It seems, therefore, a natural progression to make many of the familiar kinds as toys to play with.

2 Materials and Methods

All the basic information needed for soft toy making is given in the following two chapters. An understanding of fabrics, patterns and methods is necessary if you are to make your toys successfully. Beginners and experienced toymakers alike, who should not be beyond discovering new ideas, are advised to read carefully these pages and the individual instructions given for each toy before proceeding.

Fabrics

There are several important considerations that you should bear in mind when selecting the fabric to make your toy. First, there is the suitability of the fabric for toymaking, including its strength and washability. Then there is the suitability of the fabric to represent or complement the animal being made. However, the characteristics of colour, texture and design will be uppermost in your mind at this time. This is quite understandable, for these features, used separately or combined, will determine the response to your toy. It goes without saying that the toy with the most appeal is the one that has been carefully thought out and specially made for a particular child, with his likes and dislikes accounted for.

Lightweight fabrics such as those used for dressmaking are best kept for dolls' clothes. They are generally not strong enough to hold the shape and survive the wear and tear of play. Heavier weight dressmaking fabrics such as those used for coating and skirting can be used successfully for making toy skins. The majority of dinosaurs and dragons have been made from soft furnishing weight fabrics. These tend to be printed in much bolder patterns and often have hard-wearing properties incorporated in their manufacture, which makes them eminently suitable for toymaking.

Felt is used to make all the miniature toys and many of the additional features like claws, horns, plates and eyes which are sewn to the outside surface of the toy. It is an economical fabric to use in that it is sold in a very wide range of colours, has no grain and non-fraying edges. Layers of felt can be sewn edge to edge without a seam allowance, and it can also be surface stitched on to other fabrics without turnings. The greatest disadvantage is that it cannot be washed. There are different qualities of felt to choose from, and it pays to buy a firm one. If only thin quality felt is available, iron or glue on a suitable backing, such as Vilene.

Fur fabrics have a special fascination for young children, who like cuddly toys which incorporate the soft texture of fur. With this in mind, I obviously had to include furry dinosaurs in the book, even though fur does not seem at first glance to be right for scaly-textured, cold-blooded animals. Jointed toys are also more successful if made in fur fabrics, and thus the challenge became twofold. The duck-billed dinosaurs Parasaurolophus and Kritosaurus are made in fur, as is Deinosuchus, the bean bag prehistoric crocodile.

Difficult fabrics to use are those that fray easily, have a pattern dominated by stripes, checks or spots, or are constructed to allow stretch. These are all best avoided until you have gained experience.

Having outlined the properties of fabrics

which make them suitable for toymaking, it is time to consider whether they can be related to dinosaurs and dragons in any special way. Dinosaurs are popularly thought of as large and aggressive, especially if of the meat-eating kind. Dragons, on the other hand, are considered either fearsome or friendly, depending on whether they are oriental or occidental in origin. Bold colours like red, purple, emerald, orange and black can suggest aggressiveness, while pastel colours denote softness and youthfulness. In this case, colour is being used to indicate the character of the animals. Mediaeval and heraldic dragons are predominantly green, red or black. Chinese dragons are described by ancient writers as being yellow, blue, red, white and black.

Many present-day animals are recognized by specific colour patterns; for instance the black and white of pandas and zebras and the yellow and black of tigers. These colours should be incorporated into your toymaking, for they provide the identity of the animal. However, all this is of little comfort to dinosaur makers, as we have no evidence at all for any colour, let alone colour patterns. What little evidence there is of the skin of dinosaurs is concerned with its texture. Pieces of mummified material of Anatosaurus, a duck-billed dinosaur, show that the body was covered with a leathery skin, similar to that of modern crocodiles and the Gila Monster. Arranged over the skin were areas of small tubercles interspersed with clusters of larger, flat tubercles. Many fossils have been found with bony plates, thorns and spikes, all giving a clear picture of an armoured texture. Dragons are frequently likened to serpents and, since the latter are reptilian, we find that artists and historians describe them as being covered with scales and spines.

Perhaps we should look at modern reptiles and take our lead from them. These animals have a tough or scaly skin and are also cold-blooded. Colours are of every conceivable hue, from the dullest to the brightest and most gaudy. So we could be justified in using materials which denote any combination of these features. Bulky swamp herbivores like Brontosaurus and Brachiosaurus have bodies that are characterized by size, long neck and tail. Here is a perfect opportunity to use a gaily patterned fabric to stop the toy from looking like a large lump. Look at the colour photographs throughout the book to see how wide your choice might be.

Tools and Accessories

Most of the tools and accessories that you will need for making the dinosaurs and dragons in this book will already be in your dressmaking work-basket or in the household tool-box. Very little specialized equipment is needed, which probably explains why soft toy making is a relatively inexpensive craft to pursue.

General equipment includes scissors, both for fabric and card cutting, pinking shears, assorted needles for fine sewing, darning and embroidery, pins, mercerized cotton thread, such as Sylko in the UK, and Coats or Clarks in the USA, tailor's chalk, strong linen thread, tape measure, sewing machine, knitting needles, crochet hook, pliers, wire cutters, hammer and screwdriver. The purpose of using some of this equipment will become apparent as you read through the following list. Additional tools and accessories that will be needed at some time are also included.

For pattern making

large sheets of plain or squared paper
thin card
pencils and ruler
set square with right angle
pair of compasses for making circles

For stuffing

forceps and stuffing sticks (toothpicks, wooden meat skewers, dowelling rods, rulers, pencils and the handles of wooden spoons all make satisfactory stuffing sticks)

For jointing

thin, round-nosed pliers
steel knitting needle
joints
spare cotter pins

For wiring

pipe cleaners
florist's wire
no. 16 gauge galvanized wire
adhesive tape
seam tape or narrow strips of rag
wire cutters
thin, round-nosed pliers
heavy duty pliers for thicker wire

For surface decoration

embroidery threads
lurex threads
beads
sequins and sequin waste
ric rac
braid

For inserting safety lock-in eyes

special fixing tool which consists of a handle
   and four ferrules of different sizes
hammer
foam pad or folded towel to act as a cushion
   while hammering
screwdriver, pliers and wire cutters to remove wrongly inserted eyes

For inserting wired eyes

wire cutters
thin, round-nosed pliers

steel knitting needle
long darning needle

For grooming the finished toy

soft and hard brushes
damp sponge
vacuum cleaner
teasel brush

For stringing a mobile

nylon fishing line
brass rings
the eye portion of a hook and eye unit

Adhesives

With all the different types of glue now available to choose from, it becomes rather confusing to decide which glue sticks which substance best. You can use a clear resin adhesive such as Sellobond or a white PVA adhesive like Dufix or Bostick 8 to make the card rolls for the puppets. These give fairly fast bonds and are clean to use. For gluing fabrics, a rubber-based adhesive such as the white latex of Copydex is ideal, as the bond remains flexible. More important, toys incorporating Copydex can be washed, boiled, brushed, vacuumed and ironed with a cool to warm iron. The toys must not be dry cleaned. Another glue suitable for bonding felt and fabrics is Bostick clear adhesive No. 1. Both the above fabric glues will also bond paper and card. With this in mind, it is possible to use one glue for all the tasks undertaken in the book. My own preference is for Copydex.

Patterns, Layouts and Cutting

The pattern for any toy in this book is printed on a squared grid. Before you can proceed to make a toy it will be necessary to enlarge the pattern diagram so that you have a full-size workable copy. Careful pattern making is essential if you are to make a toy that will fit together neatly and, when finished, be the same size as that given in the instructions.

To make these patterns you will need large sheets of paper marked with a similar grid. The grid scale is marked on the pattern graph. You can buy paper ready marked with a grid from stationers, or dressmakers' pattern paper from the sewing departments of large stores. If this is not convenient, then make your own by ruling the lines and using a set square to get right angle corners.

Now carefully copy the pattern shapes from the squared grid on to the same number of squares on your ruled paper. Make sure that your pencil outline crosses the grid line in exactly the same place as that on the pattern diagram. It is only by doing this that you will finish with a correctly-shaped pattern (see Figure 1). If you are copying a large pattern shape, it might be helpful to number the squares both horizontally and vertically. This will make easy reference points to check against.

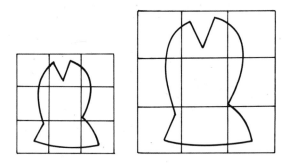

Figure 1 Preparation of pattern

In many cases, where both sides of a pattern piece are the same, only half of it will be drawn on the pattern graph. The other half is indicated by the 'place on fold' sign. First you must enlarge the half pattern by the method already outlined. Then lay fold edge of pattern to a folded piece of paper and cut around the unfolded edge. Unfold the paper and you have the full-size pattern piece.

Where an underbody gusset carefully duplicates the outline of the side body, then these pieces of pattern will be superimposed on each other, the smallest part being

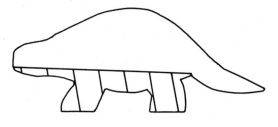

Figure 2 Pattern of side body showing superimposed underbody

shaded by diagonal lines (see Figure 2). To make full-size copies of both pieces you need only enlarge the side body pattern. Now cut a duplicate paper copy and mark the edge of the underbody gusset on it, then cut away the unwanted portion of the side body. You will not only save time doing it this way, but will also find that the legs fit together perfectly.

A long-tailed and long-necked dinosaur may well have the pattern diagram broken into sections for easy positioning on the squared grid. You must join all the enlarged sections together before laying the pattern on fabric (see Figure 3).

Transfer all details like darts, eye, mouth and opening positions on to your pattern. Note the number of pieces to be cut and the direction in which they are to be laid on the fabric. This is indicated by the arrow. Felt has no grain, therefore pieces to be cut from felt will not have any arrows.

All pattern pieces have a seam allowance of 6 mm ($\frac{1}{4}$ in) included unless stated otherwise.

Figure 3 Pattern for body presented in three sections

If you want to be able to use your patterns again and again then I suggest you glue them to thin card. Another advantage of this is that you can draw around card patterns with a soft pencil and so avoid using pins. This is advisable when making fur fabric toys, as pins can so easily be lost in the pile. Keep all pattern pieces together

14

in large envelopes and write the amount of fabric required and sewing notions on the outside for easy reference.

How to enlarge or reduce a pattern

Reducing or enlarging patterns allows you to make families of toys and also gigantic monsters. The latter are particularly appealing to little boys, and your efforts will be well rewarded. To enlarge or reduce, you alter the scale of the grid on to which the pattern is being copied. For example, when enlarging, increase the grid scale and make the pattern by the procedure already outlined. To reduce the finished size of the toy, you decrease the scale of the grid. Remember also to increase or reduce those pieces of pattern not included in the pattern graph. A word of warning, however: to make a toy twice the size suggested, you will need upwards of four times as much material and the resulting toy will be eight times as big in volume. So proceed with modest changes, say in the order of 6 mm ($\frac{1}{4}$ in) in either direction.

Pattern layouts and cutting

The amount of fabric needed to make a toy is listed in the Materials section of the relevant chapter, whilst any special pattern or cutting instructions are given in the Cutting section. There will generally be enough to match any design on the fabric, but if you really want to be sure about this, allow a little extra when buying.

Some fabrics will need a little preparation before patterns can be laid on them. Towelling must be washed, because it shrinks. Creases and folds need to be washed or ironed out of others. The fabric for making Tyrannosaurus and Stegosaurus must be opened out and cut in half, widthways. The two pieces can then be laid together with either right or wrong sides facing, whichever is preferable for cutting. This way you will not have to join material to get a piece large enough to make the main part of the body.

Follow the general rules of layout for fabrics with or without nap. Fabrics with nap have the pattern pieces laid so that the arrows lie parallel to the selvedge edge. For fabrics with nap, such as velvet, towelling, corduroy and fur fabrics, first find the direction of the nap (pile) by stroking. Mark this direction on the back of the fabric with a large pencilled arrow. Now lay the pattern pieces on the back of the fabric with all the arrows running in the same direction. The direction of the fur pile in furry toys should follow that found in nature, that is, back from the nose, up the ears, down the body and limbs and out to the tip of the tail. When working with velvet, decide which way you want the pile to run: upwards for a rich effect or downwards so that less dirt will get ingrained. Whichever direction you choose, be consistent. Fabrics such as felt, Vilene and foam sheeting have no grain, therefore arrange the pattern pieces as closely together as possible, fitting them in rather like a jigsaw.

When cutting a pair of anything, say a body, remember to reverse the pattern to get a right and a left side (see Figure 4).

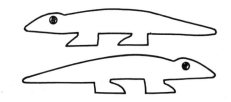

Figure 4 Right and left sides of a lizard body

Pin pattern pieces around the edge on lightweight fabrics, while on heavyweight and napped fabrics draw around the pattern pieces with a pencil or tailor's chalk. Never use pins on fur, as they constrict the fabric and also might accidentally be lost in the pile, forgotten for the moment and remembered too late. When cutting fur, move the scissors carefully between the pile so that you cut only the backing.

Never cut through double layers of fabric with nap.

Transfer any special markings to the fabric with tailor's tacks before putting away the pattern.

Stitching

All seams need to be firm enough to withstand the pressure of stuffing. This can be achieved either by hand sewing or by using a machine. However, the very large toys would simply take too long to sew by hand, and the miniature toys would be too small to fit under a machine foot. These small felt toys, the miniatures, are all hand sewn on the outside, where the seam allowance is simply the width of the stitch or 3 mm ($\frac{1}{8}$ in), depending on which stitch you use. The edges can be oversewn (see Figure 5, part 1), double oversewn (see Figure 5, part 2) or stab stitched (see Figure 5, part 3) together. Slightly larger toys can be stitched on the wrong side with a firm backstitch (see Figure 5, part 4). The very large toys can only be successfully made if a machine is used. The seams should be sewn double throughout or reinforced at least in weak areas, like corners and long, gentle curves. Make sure that you use the right size of needle and the correct thread for the fabric.

It would be advisable for beginners to tack or baste pieces together to get a good fit before sewing. Use a running stitch on lighter weight fabrics and a long oversewing stitch on fur fabrics. Tuck the pile in on the fur seams and leave these stitches in as a finishing to the seams. Experienced toy-makers must decide for themselves whether to tack long gussets or not. Tacking is otherwise only specifically mentioned when an accurate fit is required to stop a toy being lopsided, or when two pieces need easing together.

Finishing seams

A 6 mm ($\frac{1}{4}$ in) seam will not require any trimming or finishing on a straight or gently curved seam. Tight curves and curved darts should be trimmed parallel to the stitching, not clipped, as the latter is apt to break the stitching. Sharp corners need clipping to release the tension on the skin when it is turned right side out. These points are marked on the pattern by solid triangles (see Figure 6). Seams that cross over each other will need clipping. The edges of the stuffing opening may need reinforcing if they are likely to fray during a lengthy stuffing operation. Lastly, iron or finger press open any seams that need flattening, especially those on the clothes of glove puppets.

Top stitching

In dressmaking, top stitching is used to give a decorative effect to the surface of a

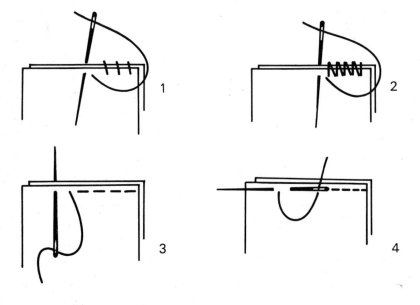

Figure 5 Some ideas for hand sewn seams 1 oversewing 2 double oversewing 3 stab stitch 4 backstitch

A Herd of Miniatures (*opposite*)
From top, moving clockwise : Dragon, Scelidosaurus, Polacanthus, Triceratops, Cobra, Mandasuchus, Monoclonius and Infant, Camptosaurus.

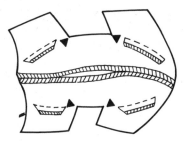

Figure 6 Underbody with clipping points marked by solid triangles

garment. In toymaking, it is used to separate adjacent areas of stuffing or to outline some significant part of the body. The fingers of Iguanodon and the toes of Dimetrodon, for example, are cut all in one, but their separate identity is provided by short rows of top stitching worked on the machine. The hands of the King are marked into fingers by handworked top stitching. The outline of the body of Pteranodon and Rhamphorhynchus is separated from the wing membranes by top stitching, and the nasal crests in the duck-billed dinosaurs have additional modelling provided by this method. You can also decide if the colour of the thread would contribute to the toy if worked in a contrasting colour.

Ladder stitch

This is the most useful of all hand-worked stitches for a toymaker. It is also essential in making professional-looking toys. Ladder stitch is used for closing the skin after stuffing, and for attaching limbs, spines, plates and horns. Using a double length of strong linen thread, make a small running stitch alternately on one side of the opening then on the other. After every three or four stitches, pull up on the thread. You will see the thread lace up the opening, automatically turning under the raw edges and leaving a smooth join (see Figure 7). When the opening is finally closed, there will be no threads on the surface for fingers to pull at or to become worn. Just as important, the threads lie parallel to the opening rather than pulling against it. Use it at all times in preference to any other stitch.

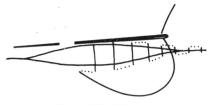

Figure 7 Ladder stitch

Ladder stitch is also the champion amongst repair stitches and in doing 'corrective surgery' to your toy. It will raise sagging parts, stop any unwanted wobbliness and brace splaying legs to the underside of a body.

Stuffing

Fillings and stuffings are determined by availability and suitability. They should ideally be lightweight, washable and hygienic. Kapok is a natural fibre that is widely available and very suitable for the miniature toys, but it is rather difficult to work with, getting on to everything rather than into the toy and it also suffers from the fact that it cannot be washed. Foam chips are also widely available and these are washable. However, they can be unattractive when they give a toy a lumpy surface. Use foam chips in fur fabric toys and in the centre of very large toys where a cushion of fibres can be packed around the chips. If using either of these fillings, work with your hands and the toy skin in the bottom of a deep bag. This stops the stuffings from spreading all over your clothes and face.

Other suitable fillings are cotton flock and all the synthetic fibres. The latter, such as polypropylene, terylene, Dacron and all the acrylics, are available from mail order firms and the larger craft shops. Deinosuchus has a filling of dried rice. Other substances which could equally well be used are beans, lentils, dried peas, millet and Polybeads.

The Horned Dinosaurs (*opposite*) *From top, moving clockwise :* Triceratops, Monoclonius, Protoceratops.

The technique of stuffing a soft toy

Having spent time sewing a skin together, it is a great pity to rush ahead with stuffing in order to get the toy finished quickly. After all, the only way to correct bad stuffing is to remove it and start again. The skin must first be prepared by trimming seams and curves, then turning through. Check that no part of the skin is under tension.

Now prepare the stuffing fibre. (Beans and chips need no such preparation.) Take a handful of fibre and tease it between your fingers to make a fluffed-up bundle. These bundles can then be inserted into the toy skin. They should be worked into the most awkward and furthermost corners first, gradually working them back towards the body proper and the stuffing opening. Pack the stuffing firmly, ramming it home with a stuffing stick. Work carefully and methodically, turning the toy from side to side to check evenness and always moulding it as work proceeds. A toy is stuffed when you are unable to push your fingers into it. I like to leave large toys at this stage, preferably resting overnight so that the stuffing has time to settle. If any further gaps appear by morning, then it is an easy matter to stuff them. Close the opening with ladder stitch.

The success of a toy depends on careful stuffing, for without sufficient stuffing, necks will not support heads, limbs wobble, joints will not work and the appearance will generally be poor.

Wiring

Wiring is used for adding strength to a soft toy and for maintaining a particular stance. Even with a limited knowledge of dinosaurs and dragons it should be obvious that many long necks and tails, tall thin legs and horns are going to need wires if the animal is to be made as a soft toy. This is the time when you must seriously consider the suitability of such a toy for a child. It is generally the older children who will be familiar with dinosaurs and request them as toys, but older children have younger brothers and sisters and these children learn all about dinosaurs at an early age. Wired toys like Brontosaurus are really not suitable for them and must never accompany them to bed. The wired feet of Tyrannosaurus are a much safer proposition, providing of course that the child can lift the toy and is strong enough to manoeuvre it through a doorway. Do make toys with the future owner in mind – it can save a lot of heartache.

There are basically two methods of making wire skeletons, which rather depend on the size of the toy being made. Very small toys, like the miniatures Cobra and Lizard, have a felt skin sewn around a wire. This sewing is done on the outside of the toy and stuffing may or may not be placed around the wire as the felt is sewn. Larger toys have the skin sewn on the inside, and are turned right side out. A prepared skeleton is inserted into the toy and is then completely embedded in a cushion of stuffing (see Figure 8).

Technique for preparing a wire skeleton

The length of wire needed for the skeleton is determined by measuring the parts to be wired, then doubling this length. This wire is cut and bent into shape so that a double thickness framework is formed. The two cut ends should lie away from the neck or feet (see Figure 8). Now wind these wires

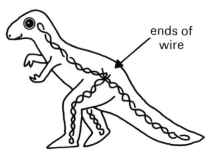

Figure 8 Position of skeletal wire in a toy dinosaur

together by holding the cut ends with pliers and placing a nail in the loop, at the bottom of a leg or in the head, so that it becomes a key.

The wires must be bound with 12 mm ($\frac{1}{2}$ in) adhesive tape, especially the cut ends. Twist long streamers of stuffing over the tape and hold in place with strong thread or knitting wool. The amount of stuffing should be as generous as the space inside the toy will permit. It need not even be of uniform thickness. Bind the stuffing with seam tape or strips of rag and catch the edges of the tape with slip stitch (see Figure 9). Some toymakers wrap the wires in collars of thin foam sheeting. Decide which method you prefer and work accordingly.

Not all toys require a complete skeleton. Figure 10 shows two different ways of making a wire skeleton for Brontosaurus. In one case the skeleton is continuous and in the other it is in two parts. The back legs are supported by a simple inverted U-shaped bridge. This will provide sufficient strength for the dinosaur to stand and to hold the tummy off the floor.

Pipe cleaners come ready prepared, cushioned in their own stuffing.

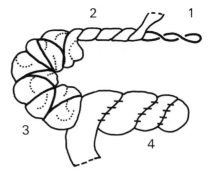

Figure 9 Preparation of skeletal wire
1 Cut end of wire turned back and twisted against main shaft   2 Adhesive tape bound over wires
3 Cushion of stuffing held in place with thread
4 Seam tape wound over stuffing and stitched in place

All pipe cleaners used in this book are 15 cm (6 in) long.

We have already seen how these can be used in the miniature toys. Pipe cleaners are also used to wire the toes in the flying reptiles, to make movable fingers in Iguanodon, to strengthen the horns in Triceratops and to make the fingers for dragons. Remember too that you can use millinery wires, fuse wires and even florist's wire and artist's picture-hanging copper wire. Use them wherever you think suitable for the toy that you are making.

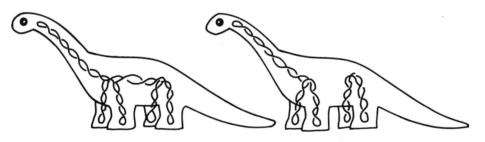

Figure 10 Skeletal wires for Brontosaurus

Jointing

The only jointed toy in the book is Parasaurolophus, although Kritosaurus could easily be adapted to accommodate joints. These dinosaurs have been made in soft fur fabric with younger children in mind. The joints enable Parasaurolophus to stand in a characteristic reptilian fashion and also to sit in a rather more familiar human way. They also make it easier for children to move the limbs during dressing and undressing. Here is an opportunity for you to design a little jacket for Parasaurolophus.

Read through the instructions first, then practise inserting a joint between two scrap

19

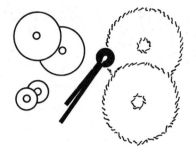

Figure 11 Joint set with a pair of fur fabric shields

pieces of material before you actually make the toy. Joints are sold in sets which consist of two hard discs – each with a central clearance hole – two steel washers and a split cotter pin (see Figure 11). The hard discs are usually cut from wood or hardboard. Sometimes plastic is used. The size range is from small 18 mm ($\frac{3}{4}$ in) joints, suitable for tiny limbs, to large 15 cm (6 in) joints for jointing heads to very large toys. Smaller joints can be made by using snap fasteners as a substitute. In addition to the tools listed on page 13 you will also need two circles of felt, leather or thick scrap material to make fabric masking shields for the joints. These should be cut 18 mm ($\frac{3}{4}$ in) larger than the hard discs. They will mask and conceal the joint from the outside of the toy and, just as important, help to reduce wear and tear on the fabric of the limb which results from the friction of a moving joint (see Figure 12).

Always use the largest joint possible to fit into the jointing position.

Technique of limb jointing

The technique of jointing is presented in a series of easy-to-follow stages. Remember that the method for all limbs, whether arms or legs, is similar. Figure 12 shows a completed joint with all the various parts locked in position.

1 Dismantle the joint set into separate components.
2 Cut and sew the limb, leaving the top, that is the hip or shoulder, open.
3 Turn limb right side out and stuff nearly to the top.
4 Pierce the position of the joint in the limb fabric with a knitting needle, to make a hole for the cotter pin. This position is marked on the pattern.
5 Take the split cotter pin and, holding the eye between your fingers, thread on to the tail end a steel washer, hard disc and a fabric shield, in that order.
6 Now push cotter tail through the joint position prepared in Stage 4.
7 Finish stuffing the limb, packing it firmly around the head of the joint, and close the hip or shoulder opening with ladder stitch.
8 The limb is now ready for jointing to the body. Make sure that you have prepared a pair of limbs.
9 Pierce a hole in the wall of the body at the joint position, which is again marked on the pattern.
10 Push the tail end of the cotter, projecting from the finished limb, through this hole.
11 Thread on to the cotter tail, a fabric shield, wooden disc and a steel washer, in that order.
12 Now lay the toy on a table so that the limb is against the table and the body is uppermost. Hold the disc firmly between your fingers, pressing down on the table. Alternatively, you may prefer to pinch the pieces of the joint together between your fingers and thumb.
13 Split the arms of the cotter pin apart and take one arm of the tail between your thin-nosed pliers. Then at the same time as you pull it up firmly, turn the arm over and bend it down sharply against the disc.
14 Pull and turn the other arm of the cotter in the same way.

The pull on the cotter must be maintained

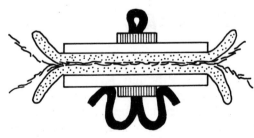

Figure 12 Cross section of a joint locked in position

20

while you are turning the tail down. This draws all the pieces of the joint tightly together, while the turning locks it into position. If you follow these stages carefully you will make really firm joints which will last indefinitely. Joints have a natural tendency to work loose over a long period of time, so you can see why it is important to start with firm joints. If you have inserted a weak joint, now is the time to take it out and remake the joint. Occasionally a cotter pin will snap with the additional bending. For this reason it is advisable to keep spare cotters in your work-box.

3 Finishing Techniques

A beautifully finished toy, full of expression and character, is very appealing and much loved even if it is, alas, poorly put together. On the other hand, a carefully made toy that is finished in a hurry with little or no regard for character will be unappealing, unloved and all too often banished to the bottom of the toy-box. What a pity if this were to happen to any of the toys you make.

So pause a while here and consider what you can learn. Always be on the look out for new ideas and never be afraid to experiment, for the character and individuality that you give to your toy will create a personality quite unlike that of any manufactured toy.

Needlemodelling

Just occasionally, some special contouring on the finished surface of a toy will be needed to highlight a particular feature or to accentuate the correct shape. This fabric sculpturing can be achieved by needlemodelling. All that is needed is a strong thread and a long needle. Small stitches are taken right through the toy from side to side and pulled tightly. The pulling forms hollows and ridges or bumps. Eyes that are stitched and pulled tightly into the head are in fact making needlemodelled sockets at the same time, and thereby giving the face more character.

Ankylosaurus has a needlemodelled tail and Yaleosaurus has needlemodelled feet. These are just two examples of localized needlemodelling. There are many others, and it is really up to you to take a critical look at your toys and decide whether this technique would improve their appearance. The King and his daughter, the Princess, provide a wonderful opportunity for you to see just what you can do with this method. The entire facial features of eyes, nose, mouth, cheeks and chin are raised by needlemodelling from a ball of stuffing. No two heads could ever be the same.

Decorative Stitchery and Beadwork

Rather dull, unpatterned fabrics can be made more interesting if they are decorated in some way which also contributes to the character. This is especially so with the Herd of Miniatures, where stitches and beads are used to suggest scaly skins, warty textures, armour plate, crests and horns. Embroiderers will have no trouble in working out decorative schemes of their own, while there will be some toymakers who are not at all familiar with finishing their toys in this way. Here are just a few simple ideas to start you on your way. More are given in Chapter 4, and reference to embroidery guides will produce a whole range of possibilities.

Sequins and beads

Sequins make perfect scales for little toys, as they are the right size. In addition they

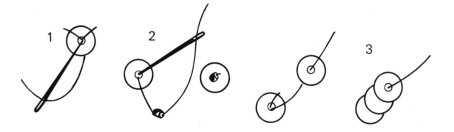

Figure 13 Attaching sequins 1 By thread 2 By using a small bead 3 By making a row

have a lovely metallic or iridescent shine which is indicative of reptilian skins. Just look at some colour plates in books of snakes to see how true this is. They can be sewn on either separately or in rows. The single sequins are held in position by several stitches or by using a little bead in the centre (see Figure 13). The latter combination is also useful for making small eyes, as a dark-coloured bead becomes the pupil on a light-coloured sequin.

Sequins may be flat, cupped, ridged and even cut in decorative shapes. There are also some very large varieties which can be quite exciting to use. Sequins are stamped out of a narrow metallic band and this band, covered with holes, is sold from large bead shops as sequin waste. You will see that I have used it in Chapter 4 to decorate the wings of the Dragon.

Little beads can be scattered over felt to indicate a knobbly texture. Slightly larger beads can be used as eyes, and they may need a little spot of white paint or white felt on them to make a highlight. When I was buying a selection of beads to decorate

these toys, I found some clear plastic banana-shaped beads and immediately thought how useful they would be as spines and horns if only they were coloured. So I dipped them in a non-toxic enamel paint (Airfix). This paint can be bought in very small pots, from toy shops and some stationers as well as craft and hobby shops.

Never use a lead-based paint in your toy-making.

Thread a pin through the hole in the bead and then hold the tail end of the pin while you dip it in the paint. Drain the bead over the pot then pin the bead into a styrofoam ball and leave it to dry overnight.

Stitchery

There must be as many different stitches as there are beads, and you will no doubt have your favourites. Use stranded embroidery cotton, which you can separate into any number of strands from one to six, although three is generally sufficient. The thread is lustrous and quite suitable for all types of

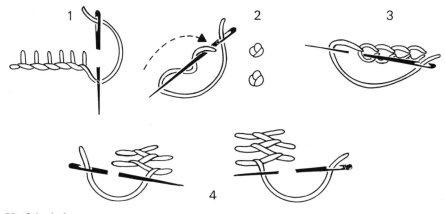

Figure 14   Useful stitches
1 Buttonhole stitch   2 French knots   3 Chain stitch   4 Cretan stitch – two stages of formation

23

stitchery. Figure 14 shows some stitches that you will be able to use for decoration.

Stitchery and beadwork can also be combined; for instance, by sewing little beads into the loops formed by working chain stitch. On the other hand, French knots could take the place of little beads. *Coton à broder* and lurex threads are also worth considering in your decoration.

Lastly, a word about ric rac. It has been used to form the crested back in many of the toys. Remember that you can buy it in several widths and that there are also lurex varieties. Figure 15 shows some of the ways that you can sew ric rac to other fabrics.

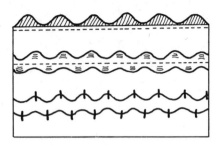

Figure 15 Ideas for using ric rac

Character-Making Features

The most satisfying part of toymaking is that moment when you give character to your toy and bring it to life. Any number of toymakers using the same pattern will impart some of themselves at this stage and, for this reason, no two toys will ever be finished the same way. Whether your toy looks happy or sad, friendly or ferocious, intelligent or stupid, will depend on how you make and position those emotional features that create character. There is a narrow dividing line between a toy that looks right and one that looks wrong. It may simply be the relationship of features to one another, features that contribute enormously to the success and appeal of a toy; take care when you are character-making.

Eyes

These are the most important of all character-making features. Used alone, that is without mouth, teeth, claws or nostrils, they can create any of the expressions mentioned above, and many more. When selecting eyes, consider the type to be used, and the size and position they should have on the head. We know from the skulls of dinosaurs where the eyes were positioned. Modern reptiles display an enormous variety of eyes, reflecting their many different ways of life. There are large, bulbous eyes, small, beady eyes, colours of every description, including bright red, and pupils that may be as narrow as slits. Then there are the eye cones of the chameleon, which move independently of each other and keep the glint from their prey until the last possible moment. They also have eyelids capable of closing to tiny peepholes. Burrowing lizards, which live in the dark with little need for vision have no more than tiny 'dot' eyes in the skin. Alligators have pupils that are reminiscent of those in cats.

Eyes for dragons can be as varied as you like, for they are imaginary animals. The eyes of the puppet people should present no problems. Observe people around you to see where they are positioned, and the wealth of expression that can be had from them. Youthfulness can be indicated by positioning them low down on the face and slightly more than their own width apart. Eyes that are too close together give a mean-looking individual, and those too high on the head make a puppet or toy animal appear senseless. There are anatomical explanations for all these phenomena; for example, there is no room for a brain if the eyes are placed too high – hence the senseless expression.

Another factor that you should bear in mind is the mode of life of the animal being made. Is the animal a hunter with forward-facing and keen eyes? Is the animal one that lives on land and in the water and has raised eyes like phytosaurs, crocodiles and the large swamp herbivores?

24

There are basically two types of eyes to choose from. Firstly, there are the commercially produced plastic eyes with safety washers, and the wired glass eyes. Secondly, there are all the hand-made eyes that may incorporate fabric, felt, buttons, beads and embroidery. This second category offers an opportunity to make distinctive eyes beyond the scope of plastic and glass eyes.

Felt can be cut to any shape and size and is available in virtually every colour imaginable. The various parts of eye background, iris, pupil and highlight can be arranged to give the exact expression required. Highlights may be worked with a small block of satin stitches, a few shiny sequins or even a dab of white paint. All the separate parts are best glued or stitched together first so that you make a complete eye, which can then either be glued or stitched to the head as a single unit. Deinosuchus has large bulbous eyes made by gathering a circle of felt and enclosing a knob of stuffing in it to give shape. Lizard and Dimetrodon have the eye stitched flat to the skin, enclosing a small layer of stuffing, which raises it.

Many of the toys have buttons for their eyes and I would strongly recommend a shopping expedition to your nearest store with a large button counter. The buttons can be used alone or in conjunction with a felt background. Many will have a shank at the back by which they are sewn to clothing. Now in toymaking, a button of this type would wobble on the surface if it were not treated first to make it more suitable. One method is to tie double button thread on to the shank, then sew these threads through to the opposite side of the head and tie them off very tightly. Pull at the same time as you tie off, so that you form a socket for the eye to rest in. Another method is to use the button as the pupil only and to cut a layer of felt for an eye background. Punch a hole in the centre of the felt and push the shank through. Now build up the back of the eye by cutting smaller circles of felt and punching holes in them in the same way. Thread these over the shank until felt and shank are level (see Figure 16). Sew the felt and shank together to hold in place. The completed unit can now be glued or stitched to the head. The

effect of all the additional felt pieces behind the button is to stop wobbling and also to raise it.

Figure 16 Shank button used as an eye. The largest felt oval forms the eye background while the three smaller ovals are used to build up the back

Safety lock-in eyes range in size from 6 mm to 24 mm, and are generally only used in fur fabric toys. Several different types of tool are available for inserting them, the handle with magnetized ferrules being preferable. Follow the instructions provided with each tool. Once a safety eye is inserted, it is quite impossible to remove, apart from cutting it out, so you must be sure of its position before you proceed. Never take the eye position marked on a pattern for granted; always check first. Uneven sewing will quickly alter the position and therefore possibly ruin the required character.

To insert safety lock-in eyes using the handle tool, you first position them on the outside of a lightly-stuffed head. Mark the required position with a soft pencil. Now make a hole in this position with a knitting needle or the point of a small pair of scissors, just large enough to admit the shank of the eye. Empty out the stuffing from the head. Insert shank from the right side of fabric and place washer in position with the fixing tool. The eye should be protected during this stage by resting it on a foam pad. Now tap the washer home firmly with a hammer. When inserted, there should be no space between eye, fabric and washer. Knitted fur fabrics may need a protective felt patch glued on the inside to stop the stitches of the fabric from running when you make the hole for the shank.

Glass eyes are sold in pairs connected by a length of wire (see Figure 17). The size range is the same as that given for safety eyes. Separate the eyes by cutting the wire 18 mm ($\frac{3}{4}$ in) from each eye. Bend the wire into a shank with thin-nosed pliers. Make sure that the end of the wire is closed tightly around the base of the shank.

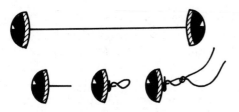

Figure 17 Preparation of glass eyes

Thread a double length of strong button thread, or even string, through the loop and tie on with a firm knot. Make a hole in the face in the eye position. Thread one set of threads on to a needle and take through this hole to the other side of the head. Repeat with the remaining set of threads. Pull on all the threads and tie off tightly, then darn the ends away into the head before cutting. For forward facing eyes, the threads can be tied off at the neck, and for sideways facing eyes, the threads are best tied off behind the opposite eye. Whichever direction the threads take, always pull on them tightly, so that the shank passes through the fabric, leaving only the eye on the surface. The tension on the threads will form eye sockets, which provide additional shaping to the face.

Eyelashes and eyebrows

Eyelashes are not a feature of dinosaurs yet, when added to a fierce animal, they will soften the expression and make it appear more friendly and cuddly. Just imagine what a set of long, curly lashes would do for Tyrannosaurus! At the same time, be careful not to overdo it, as it is not in our nature to think of Tyrannosaurus as a family favourite.

Eyelashes are also used to indicate feminity, especially if you embroider them. Make the eyelashes for animals from fringed felt. Eyebrows can be used as character-making features, for instance the green lids of the King make him look rather sad and heavy-eyed. Some of the animals have eyebrows, to stop the eye from being too stark. A glance at the photographs in the book will provide you with ideas.

Mouths

This probably brings to mind pictures of wide, gaping mouths, snapping jaws, rows and rows of sharp, pointed teeth, poisonous fangs and barbed tongues – all rather aggressive features and somewhat difficult to transfer to toys. A large, gaping mouth looks both awkward and unbalanced and for this reason is best indicated in a shut position by a row of stitching. Snapping jaws like those of dragons, crocodiles and alligators, make a wonderful movement for glove puppets, providing plenty of character as well as amusement. Teeth are always a problem in soft toy making. They are difficult to make on small toys, let alone to do it in scale. Best to use white felt, white plastic or stitching to indicate their presence, and leave it at that. Just imagine trying to fit the equivalent of 200 15 cm (6 in) pointed teeth into the mouth of Tyrannosaurus! It is the shape of the teeth that is character-making; pointed for a fierce meat-eater, and bluntened for a more docile vegetarian. The fangs of a snake can be made by stuffing felt shapes with pipe cleaners, then bending these to a characteristic curve.

Most of the toy animals have no mouth, and this in no way detracts from their character. In fact, a mouth worked on a highly-coloured and patterned fabric could be both difficult to see and confusing. Decide for yourself whether your fabric and toy need a mouth. Use a mouth to indicate happiness by turning up the corners into a smile. Sadness is a downward-curved mouth, while meanness is a tight, thin mouth. Do be careful not to give a monster a leering look unless particularly desired.

The beard surrounding the mouth of the King suggests an elderly person, and by making it from white dish cloth cotton or wool, the character is thus positively determined. The Princess, on the other hand, has no mouth. At various times during the play she would be either sad or happy, and no single mouth could indicate these extremes of expression.

If a toy or puppet has an open mouth, then you may consider putting a tongue in it. This complements the mouth rather more than it adds character to the toy. On the other hand, some animals have very striking tongues, which serve to identify

26

them. There are, for example, the barbed tongues of dragons and the forked tongues of snakes; then there is the very long, sticky tongue of a chameleon. Several toys in the book have open mouths, and you will find tongues made of felt, lightly-padded shapes and even picture wire.

Noses and nostrils

These are usually added at the same time as the mouth, but with the toys in this book a clear distinction must be made between noses and nostrils. Nevertheless, both can be important in determining the character of the toy. Noses are more frequently associated with human beings, and animals like cats, dogs, lions, bears and rabbits; while only nostrils are found in other groups like fish, reptiles and animals derived from them, such as dragons and serpents.

Noses are usually worked to cover a well-defined area of the face, while nostrils may be simply represented by two dots signifying the two small openings, or more conspicuously in the dragons, where their presence contributes to the character of an aggressive, fire-breathing animal. Nostrils are not always at the front of the head; for example, the giant amphibious sauropods Diplodocus and Brachiosaurus and the phytosaurs have nostrils opening on top of their heads above the eyes, which probably enabled them to breathe while they were submerged. This is rather similar to the high bulbous nostrils of crocodiles and hippopotamuses, which function in the same way.

Perhaps the strangest of all developments was that found in the duck-billed dinosaurs, where the bones of the head produced a wide variety of crests. Some of these were solid, while others were hollow. Those that were hollow contained the air passages which passed from the nostrils to the throat. You can see these crests in Parasaurolophus and Kritosaurus.

Claws, spines, plates and crests

The size, shape and arrangement of these features are a means of identification for many of the dinosaurs, often distinguishing between very similar animals. They may be added to a toy either during the make-up, or later, at the finishing stage. In addition, the very nature of claws, spines and armour suggests aggression and defence and will obviously contribute enormously to the character. The most popular method of making small spines and claws is to cut them from felt, because it is a non-fraying material. These can then be sewn on to the outer surface of a toy during the finishing stage. Larger plates and crests can be cut from the body fabric and sewn into the toy during the make-up stage. Nearly every dinosaur and dragon in the book has some of these features, and you will find that there are many different ways of working them. However, you may well develop some methods for yourself or even interchange methods between the toys. This is where you should experiment, for the more monstrous your monster, the more he will be loved by the children.

4   A Herd of Miniatures

Miniature toys have a fascination of their own, and this felt dinosorium is no exception. All the animals are hand sewn, and are therefore suitable for young children and beginners to make.

Cobra

Cobras are amongst the most dangerous snakes known to mankind, being very venomous. When threatened, they rear up, spread their necks into a menacing flattened 'hood' and accompany all this with a loud hissing noise.

Materials: 3 pipe cleaners
23 cm (9 in) square of felt
very small amount of stuffing
2 beads for eyes
30 sequins
12 bugle beads
gold lurex thread for tongue

Cutting: Cut a length of felt 17·5 × 2·5 cm (7 × 1 in) for the body, and a 'hood' shape from the diagram. This makes a snake 17·5 cm (7 in) long, although he will be less than this if coiled.

Twist the three pipe cleaners together and lay on the body strip of felt. Push them up close to one end of the felt, then roll the felt around the pipe cleaners. Starting at one end, slip stitch the edge of the felt to the roll and work along the length. The felt is just longer than the pipe cleaners, which allows you to put a little stuffing in at the end to make a head area. Lay the hood over the head, using Figure 18 as a guide. Work

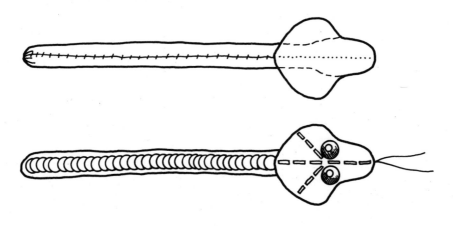

Figure 18 Construction of Cobra showing position of hood and decorative beadwork

a few tiny stitches at the front and back of the hood to hold it in place. Sew on two beads for eyes, which will also hold the hood in place. The Cobra is now ready for decoration. Cover the seam with a row of sequins, which hide the slip stitches, and decorate the hood with a pattern of bugle beads. Sew two strands of lurex thread at the front to make a forked tongue. The Cobra can now be coiled into any position.

You could use this same pattern to make any other species of snake by simply omitting the hood. Felt could be used for the eyes instead of shiny beads, and you may prefer to decorate the body with stitchery.

Mandasuchus

This small reptile was an ancestor of the dinosaurs, belonging to the same group that gave rise to crocodiles, dinosaurs, flying reptiles and birds. Mandasuchus was rather similar to a crocodile in size and build, with a double row of armour plates down its back.

Materials:
5 pipe cleaners
14 g ($\frac{1}{2}$ oz) double knitting (thick) wool
23 cm (9 in) square of felt
23 cm (9 in) ric rac
2 beads for eyes
embroidery thread for mouth and nostrils

Cutting:
Make a pattern from the pattern graph. Do not fringe the feet and hands until you have stitched them. This makes a toy 15 cm (6 in) long.

Take a pipe cleaner and bend it in half. Lay a second pipe cleaner in the bend, then bind the wool over the two pipe cleaners, building up the shape seen in Figure 19. This makes a trunk and head shape which you can now lay on the body felt. Leave the head projecting from the longer of the two straight edges. Roll the edges of the felt over the body so that you have a join in the centre of the back. Slip stitch this edge, then cover it with a length of ric rac. If by any chance you haven't wound sufficient wool, simply trim the edges of the felt to make them smaller or insert a little stuffing.

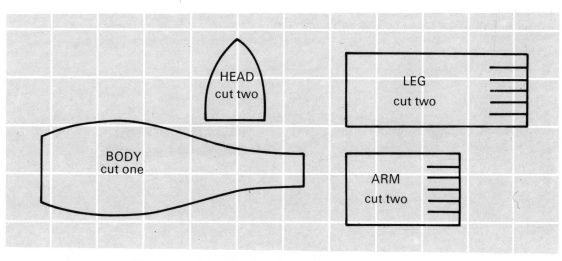

Pattern graph 1   Mandasuchus *one square = 2·5 cm (1 in)*

Oversew the two head pieces together, then turn right side out. Push the bound head into the felt head and add extra stuffing, if needed. Gather up the neck edges of the head and body and sew them together. Cover the join with a collar of ric rac. Sew on two beads for the eyes and work a mouth and nostrils with embroidery thread.

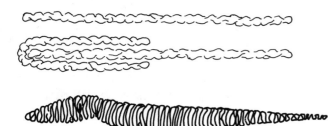

Figure 19 How to fold the pipe cleaners and make the body shape for Mandasuchus

Take a pipe cleaner and bend it in half, lay on a leg strip of felt beyond the fringed area. Roll the felt over the pipe cleaner and close the edge. Work a few small stab stitches at the foot of the leg so that they hold the pipe cleaner in place. Now fringe the foot area, snipping with the points of your scissors. Bend the leg into shape, following Figure 20. Arrange the bend so that the seam lies to the inside edge, out of sight. Now stitch the bends together, along the seam. Make a second leg in the same way, taking care to make a pair. Place legs on either side of the body and catch in place with tiny stitches.

To make the front limbs, first cut a pipe cleaner in half. Now take one half and bend

it in half as you did for the leg. Lay on the felt and make in the same way. Bend the completed limb into the shape of Figure 21.

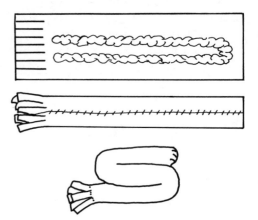

Figure 20 Construction of leg for Mandasuchus

Make the second limb so that you have a pair, then stitch both to the body. Because pipe cleaners will bend, you can position the head, body and tail of Mandasuchus in different ways. The whole body can also be raised so that the animal rests on its forelimbs, as seen in Figure 22. Make this little toy from green felt, cover it with sequins and you have a crocodile. Make it from green or red felt and add wings – now you have a serpent or dragon (see Figure 23).

Figure 21 Completed arm of Mandasuchus

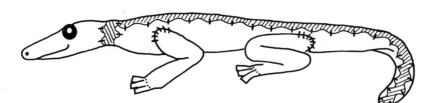

Figure 22 Mandasuchus

Figure 23 Dragon made from the pattern for Mandasuchus

Scelidosaurus

Scelidosaurus was an early ornithiscian dinosaur, having been found in the rocks of Dorset and described as long ago as 1861. The body was covered with an armour-plated skin, so it is not surprising that Scelidosaurus is regarded as an ancestral stegosaur and ankylosaur.

Materials:
23 cm (9 in) square of felt
23 cm (9 in) ric rac
28 g (1 oz) stuffing
embroidery thread
2 beads for eyes

Cutting:
Make a set of patterns from the pattern graph. This makes a toy 23 cm (9 in) long. Cut two each of side body, underbody, front and back soles.

Join the two underbodies on the wrong side from A to B. Now, working on the right side and from the head, join each side to its matching underbody. Insert the front and back soles as you come to them, then sew both sides together beyond B to the end of the tail. Sew the centre back seam with stab stitch, enclosing a length of ric rac, which

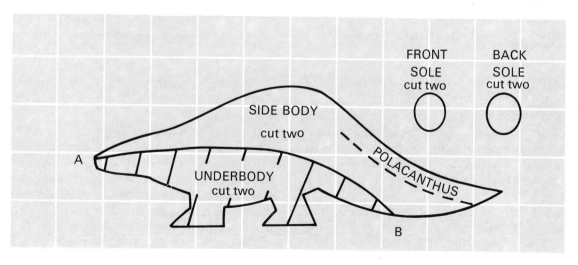

Pattern graph 2   Scelidosaurus and Polacanthus *one square = 2·5 cm (1 in)*

should reach to the neck. The skin should be stuffed at the same time as you close the back. Pay particular attention to the legs and tail, seeing that they are firm. Finish

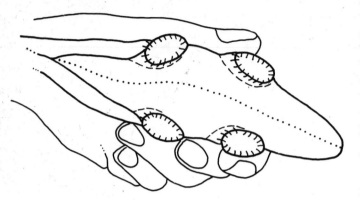

Figure 24 Scelidosaurus held in left hand to ladder stitch legs to underbody

stuffing the body and the head as you end the seam at A.

With a simple pattern like this, the legs have a tendency to splay out at an awkward angle. You can correct this tendency by turning Scelidosaurus over to rest upside down in the palm of your hand, and pushing the front legs in towards the tummy between your thumb and fingers. This will make a crease at the inside top of each leg. Now work a row of ladder stitching along either side of the crease line to hold the leg in position (see Figure 24). Repeat this procedure for all the legs, moving your fingers back when you come to the hind legs.

Decorate the sides of the body with three rows of chain stitch to represent the armour plate. Finish Scelidosaurus by sewing on the eyes.

Polacanthus

Polacanthus was an early ankylosaur, known from only one specimen which, rather unfortunately, had no head. The body had two rows of enormous spines running down the back to a tail that was covered with plates. The armour was not as complete as that found in Ankylosaurus.

Materials:
23 cm (9 in) square of felt
23 cm (9 in) ric rac
28 g (1 oz) stuffing
10 small banana-shaped beads
4 large banana-shaped beads
2 beads for eyes

Cutting:
Make a set of patterns from the pattern graph given for Scelidosaurus. Cut a slit along the line marked Polacanthus on the side. This makes a toy 23 cm (9 in) long. Cut as for Scelidosaurus.

Cut the ric rac in half and then insert a length in each slit on the tail of the side body. Stab stitch in place, keeping the tip of the tail as neat as possible. Polacanthus is then assembled in exactly the same way as already described for Scelidosaurus, except for the centre back seam, which has no ric rac.

I have used banana-shaped beads for the spines. If you are unable to buy any, try making spines from felt. Arrange the spines on either side of the back, so that there are three small spines on the shoulders, followed

by two large, then two more small spines (see Figure 25). Finish the toy by sewing on the eyes.

You could use this same pattern to make a miniature Stegosaurus. Continue the slit further forward to the shoulders and then stab stitch plates into each slit as you close it. This would give you two separate rows of plates, which is anatomically correct. The usual method for making Stegosaurus has the two rows of plates stitched in the centre back seam. Decide for yourself which design you prefer.

The Giant Plant-Eaters (*opposite*) *Left*: Brontosaurus. *Right*: Yaleosaurus.

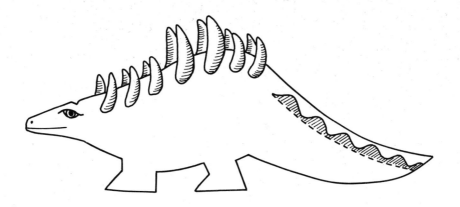

Figure 25 Position of spines on Polacanthus

Triceratops

Triceratops occurs frequently in the fossil beds of western parts of North America, and is certainly one of the most popularly known dinosaurs. Triceratops is Greek for 'three-horned face', which perfectly describes this animal, although in other respects the body resembles that of a rhinoceros.

Materials:
- 23 cm (9 in) square of felt
- 12·5 cm (5 in) ric rac
- 28 g (1 oz) stuffing
- 2 beads for eyes
- 2 large and 1 small banana-shaped beads
- 20 small beads for back

Cutting:
Make a set of patterns from the pattern graph. This makes a toy 12·5 cm (5 in) long. Cut two side bodies, one underbody, four soles, two heads and one frill from the felt.

Using stab stitch, sew a side body to the underbody. Work back from A to B and insert the soles as you come to them. Repeat with the remaining side body, then sew both together from B to the tip of the tail. Sew the centre back seam, enclosing the ric rac and stuffing the toy at the same time. End the ric rac at C, then carry on sewing forward to finish at A. Make sure that the legs and tail are firmly stuffed before you finish the seam.

Oversew the two head pieces from D to E, then turn right side out and lay against the frill, matching E to E and F to F on each side. Stab stitch from F on one side, along the outer edge to E and on to F on the other side. Pull up on the stitches every so often to form a slightly crinkled edge to the frill. Now lay the completed head on the body and catch in place from F to A (D) to F. Sew on the eyes and each of the face horns. The small horn lies above the nostrils while the two larger horns lie in the eyebrow position. Decorate the body with small beads, arranging them irregularly over the sides.

Iguanodon and the Duck-bills (*opposite*) *Left:* Iguanodon. *Centre:* Parasaurolophus. *Right:* Kritosaurus.

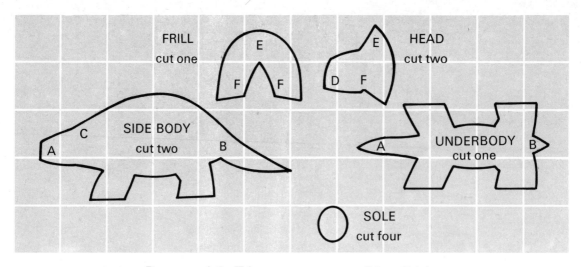

Pattern graph 3 Triceratops *one square = 2·5 cm (1 in)*

Monoclonius and Infant

During the early part of the twentieth century, Canada had a dinosaur rush along the banks of the Red Deer River, Alberta. Scientists came to collect a grand array of skeletons for their various museums and institutions. Amongst the more notable finds were the duck-billed dinosaur Corythosaurus, the carnivorous dinosaur Gorgosaurus and the horned dinosaurs Styracosaurus, Chasmosaurus and Monoclonius.

Materials: 30·5 cm (12 in) square of felt for parent
20 cm (8 in) ric rac for parent
56 g (2 oz) stuffing for parent
2 beads for parent's eyes
23 cm (9 in) square of felt for infant
28 g (1 oz) stuffing for infant
2 beads for infant's eyes
sequins and beads for decoration

Cutting: Make a set of patterns from the pattern graph for the parent. Use the pattern for Triceratops to make the infant. The parent is 20 cm (8 in) in length and the infant is the same size as Triceratops. For the parent you will need to cut two side bodies, two underbodies, two heads, one frill, one horn and four soles. Cut the infant as for Triceratops and cut a smaller horn, using the pattern for the parent as a guide.

Sew the two halves of the parent underbody together on the wrong side from A to B. Turn right side out and sew a side body to each side of the underbody. Insert the soles as you come to them. Join the two side bodies together beyond B to the tip of the tail. Close the centre back seam, enclosing a length of ric rac from C to the tip of the tail, and stuffing the toy at the same time. It is easier to work this seam from the tail forward to the head. The legs will probably splay out as they do in Scelidosaurus, so again work a row of bracing stitches along the inside top of each leg.

Follow the instructions given for Triceratops to make the frill, and sew it to the body. Fold the horn in half, matching G to G, and oversew from G to H. Turn the horn right side out, stuff and catch in place

34

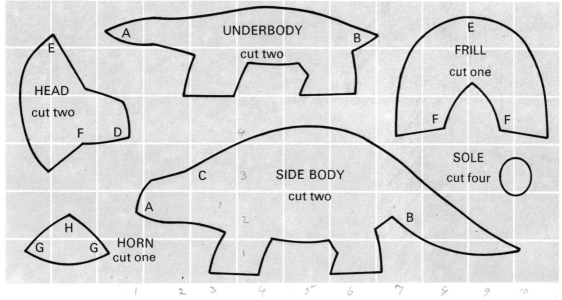

Pattern graph 4 Monoclonius and Infant *one square = 2·5 cm (1 in)*

on the head. The model of Monoclonius has the horn covered with sequin waste to decorate it. Sew on beads for the eyes or embroider them.

To make the infant Monoclonius you will need to follow the instructions given for Triceratops, omitting the ric rac from the centre back seam. Make a horn, slightly smaller than that given for the parent, and sew on to the front of the head. Both animals have the back decorated with sequins held in place by smaller beads.

You will realize by now that the parent pattern could be satisfactorily used to make a larger Triceratops. Furthermore, by altering the shape of the frill or adding horns of different sizes in different places, it is possible to make many of the horned dinosaurs. Figure 26 will give you some more ideas to try.

Figure 26 Horned dinosaurs. Use the pattern for Monoclonius to make either Styracosaurus left or Pentaceratops right

Camptosaurus

The name Camptosaurus means 'bent' or 'flexible' lizard, so called because this dinosaur could walk on its large hind legs or bend over and walk on all fours. Camptosaurus was an ancestor of Iguanodon and the duck-billed dinosaurs.

Materials: 30·5 cm (12 in) square of felt
56 g (2 oz) stuffing
2 beads for eyes
embroidery thread for stitchery
beads or sequins for decoration

Cutting: Make a set of patterns from the pattern graph. This will make a toy 12·5 cm (5 in) tall and 20 cm (8 in) long. Cut two each of side body, underbody, arm and sole pieces. Cut one underchin piece.

35

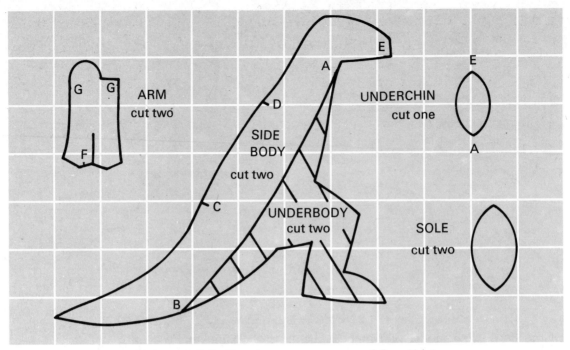

Pattern graph 5　Camptosaurus *one square = 2·5 cm (1 in)*

Sew the two underbodies together from A to B. Now sew each side body to this underbody, inserting the soles of the feet as you come to them. Join the side bodies together from B to the tip of the tail and around the back to C. Continue joining side bodies together from D, round the head to E. Insert underchin gusset, matching E to E and A to A, and sew. Stuff the skin firmly through the opening in the back, then close. Work a row of bracing stitches at the inside top of the hind legs as described for Scelidosaurus. This stops the toy from looking awkward, with widely-spaced legs.

The arms need to be made as a pair. Fold each arm in half and sew from F to G.

Stuff firmly, then sew in place on the body. Sew through the rounded, single layer of felt at the top of the arm. You can shape the arms if you wish by bending the hands and holding them with ladder stitches worked on either side of the bend.

Finish the toy by sewing on eyes, working a mouth and nostrils and decorating the body with beadwork and stitchery.

The pattern for Camptosaurus could be used to make a simple dragon. Make as described and finish by adding the wings and barbed tail of the Heraldic Dragon. You might also like to incorporate ric rac in the back seam to make a crest, and add a horn to the face.

Heraldic Dragon

Real and imaginary animals appear frequently in heraldry, with the lion as King of Beasts and the eagle as King of Birds. The only dinosaur to be used by Heralds is Iguanodon, which is emblazoned on the city Coat of Arms of Maidstone in southeast England. Dragons, especially the red and gold ones, are very popular amongst the imaginary beasts. Other strange beasts are wyverns, unicorns, gryphons and the Phoenix.

Materials:
30·5 cm (12 in) square of red felt
23 cm (9 in) square of salmon felt
7·5 cm (3 in) square of gold felt
30·5 cm (12 in) red ric rac
84 g (3 oz) stuffing
4 pipe cleaners
skein of gold embroidery thread
7·5 cm (3 in) brass picture wire
2 beads for eyes
gold sequins and beads for decoration

Cutting: Make a set of patterns from the pattern graph. The dragon is 20 cm (8 in) tall and long. From the red felt, cut two each of side bodies, wings, outside legs, arms, soles and one head gusset and nostril hood. From the salmon felt, cut two each of inside legs, arms, wings, underbody and inner ears and one only nostril. From the gold felt, cut two outer ears and two eye backings.

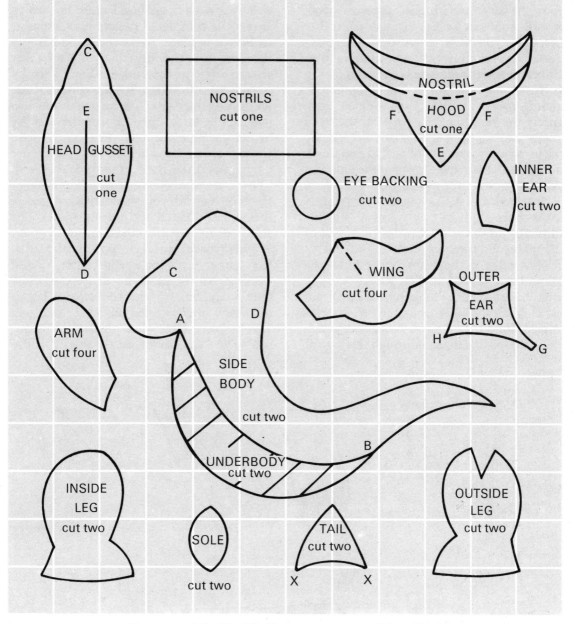

Pattern graph 6   Heraldic Dragon *one square = 2·5 cm (1 in)*

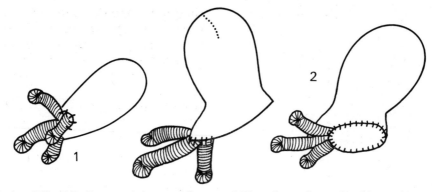

Figure 27 Limbs of Heraldic Dragon 1 Arm and fingers 2 Two views of completed leg and toes

Join the two underbodies together from A to B. Join side bodies together from B to the tip of the tail. Insert the underbody gusset and sew forward on both sides to A. Continue sewing the side bodies together to C. Insert the head gusset, matching C to C and D to D, and sew each side in turn. Insert the ric rac in the slash on the head gusset and, starting at E, stab stitch the ric rac in place, working back past D and down the centre back of the dragon to the tail. The skin must be stuffed as you close this seam.

Sew both tail pieces together, leaving X to X open. Push in tiny wisps of stuffing through this opening, then the open end of the body, and catch in place.

Now make all the limbs. Sew a red and a salmon arm piece together, leaving it open at the wrist. Stuff. Take a pipe cleaner and bend it into one long and three shorter fingers. Bind these fingers with gold thread, using a needle to thread through the loop at the top of each finger (see Figure 27, part 1). Insert the completed fingers into the wrist and catch in place. Make the second arm in the same way, checking that you have a pair with red felt to the outside. Start a leg by sewing the little dart at the top of the outside leg piece, then sew this to an inside leg, leaving the base open. Form the toes by bending a pipe cleaner into a central long toe and two outer, smaller toes (see Figure 27, part 2). Bind the toes with gold thread. Start to sew the sole into the back portion of the foot and, as you work forward, insert the toes and catch securely in place. The sole does not reach to the front of the foot, as this space is taken up by the toes. Remember to insert any last little wisp of stuffing that might be needed to make the foot really firm. Make the second leg in the same way, again checking that you have a pair. Now that all the limbs are ready, you can decide on the stance of the

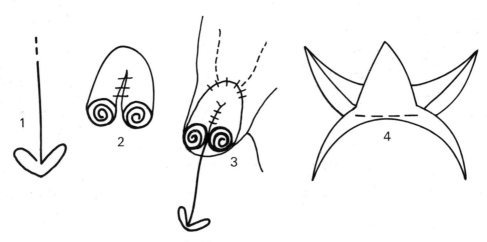

Figure 28 Construction of tongue and nose for Heraldic Dragon
1 Shape of wire to make tongue   2 Nostril felt rolled and bent into shape   3 Nostrils and tongue sewn in place   4 Construction of nostril hood

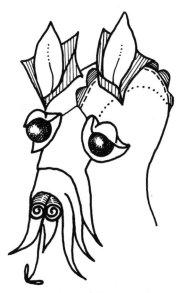

Figure 29 Head of Heraldic Dragon

toy and sew the limbs on accordingly. Use ladder stitch to do this.

Stab stitch a red and salmon wing piece together, leaving the short, straight edge open. Softly stuff the wing through this opening. Gently bend the wing in half towards the inside. This will form a crease along the line marked on the pattern. By ladder stitching along this crease you can hold the shape of the wing in a resting position. Make the other wing in the same way, then sew both to the shoulders, on either side of the ric rac in the centre back seam. It may be preferable to decorate the wings before you sew them to the body, so watch this point when designing your decoration.

Using thin-nosed pliers, take the brass wire and bend into a barbed tongue, using Figure 28, part 1, as a guide. Lay this on the snout of the dragon in a central position and securely oversew the end in place.

Roll the nostril felt into a cylinder and slip stitch the edge. Now bend into a 'U' shape and catch the two arms together (see Figure 28, part 2). Lay the two nostrils over the sewn end of the wire and catch in place (see Figure 28, part 3). Fold the nostril hood along the guide line marked on

the pattern and stab stitch close to the edge of the fold on the wrong side (see Figure 28, part 4). Lay the hood over the nostrils and forehead so that the fringed sides hang down on either side of the face and the top of the hood reaches up to E. Sew in place from F to E on each side. Figure 29 shows what the head should look like at this stage.

Take the felt eye backing and lay a bead in the centre. Sew the bead in place and fold the felt so that it forms an eyelid (see Figure 30). The completed eye unit is placed on the edge of the hood between E and F and stitched in position. Make the second eye in the same way.

Figure 30 Construction of felt eyelid over bead eye of Heraldic Dragon

Lay an inner ear on top of an outer ear and fold G over H. Sew the base, formed by three layers of felt, together, then sew the ear to the head (see Figure 31). Make the second ear in the same way.

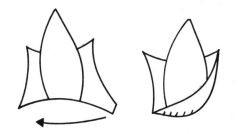

Figure 31 Construction of ear for Heraldic Dragon

Your Dragon is now ready for decoration. In the list of materials you will find that I have suggested gold sequins. These give a rich effect to your toy. Sew them on the breastplate and to the crown of the head. The wings have also been decorated with sequin waste cut to shape. Finally, bend toes and fingers to give a pleasing finish.

5   The Horned Dinosaurs

The horned dinosaurs were the last major group of dinosaurs to evolve, living about 100 million years ago. The fossil remains have been found so far only in northwest America and northeast Asia, although in these areas the remains are numerous. This suggests that they lived in herds, browsing on plants. The different species exhibited a wide range of neck frills and horns.

Protoceratops

The discovery in 1922 of the fossil remains of this animal was an outstanding event, for remains of young and adult animals and the eggs were found together in Outer Mongolia. The eggs were very similar to those of living crocodiles and, like them, were probably laid in nests dug in the ground. Protoceratops is considered the first of the horned dinosaurs, having a small frill, but no horns.

Materials:
23 cm (9 in) square of felt
25 cm ($\frac{1}{4}$ yd) of 90 cm (36 in) wide fabric
112 g (4 oz) stuffing
2 brass buttons for eyes

Cutting:
Make a set of patterns from the pattern graph. This makes a toy 10 cm (4 in) tall and 33 cm (13 in) long. Cut the head frill lining and the two inside front and hind legs from felt. All other pieces are cut from the fabric. If you are making Protoceratops for a young child, replace the buttons with felt eyes.

Place right sides of both side bodies together and sew the centre back seam. Insert the underbody gusset, matching A to A and B to B, and sew each side in turn, leaving an opening between X and X. Sew the remaining undertail seam. Turn skin right side out and stuff. Close opening. The four legs are assembled in the same way. Place a fabric and a felt pair together and sew on the wrong side. Leave a small opening for turning. Clip corners, turn, stuff and close. Position each leg on the body so that the tail sits on the floor, with the legs and the head lifted clear. Securely ladder stitch each leg in place.

Sew fabric head frill pieces together from C to D. Lay the frill lining to this and sew from C to D on each side through E. Clip corners, trim curves and turn right side out. Lay completed frill on body and catch at E on both sides. You may like to catch the hood lining to the back of the neck with a few stitches; this will hold it in place.

Sew on the buttons for eyes, pulling them in tightly to form sockets.

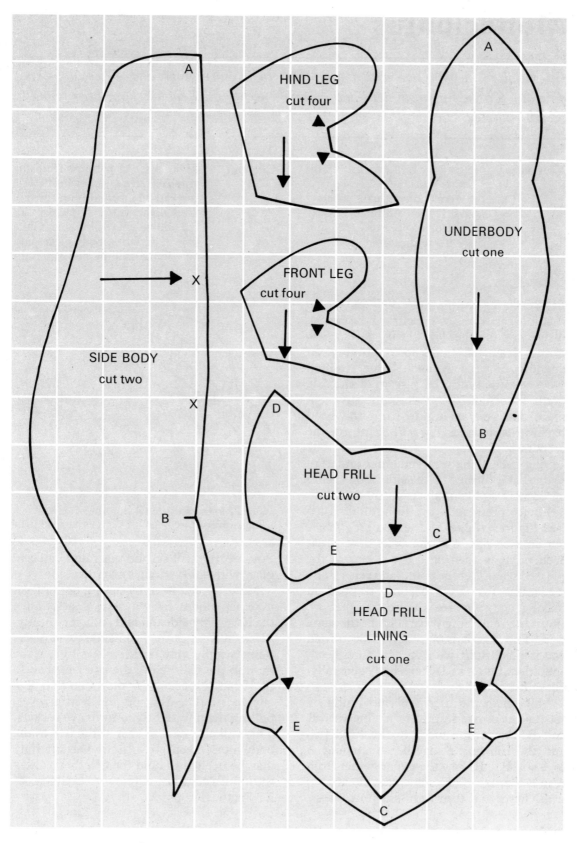

A

HIND LEG
cut four

A

UNDERBODY
cut one

X

FRONT LEG
cut four

B

SIDE BODY
cut two

X

D

HEAD FRILL
cut two

B

C

E

D

HEAD FRILL

LINING

cut one

E

E

C

Pattern graph 7   Protoceratops *one square = 2·5 cm (1 in)*

41

Monoclonius

Intermediate in both size and development to Protoceratops and Triceratops, this dinosaur has only a single horn and a simple neck frill. Remains have been found in North America.

Materials:
50 cm (½ yd) of 120 cm (48 in) wide fabric
30·5 cm (12 in) square of felt
340 g (12 oz) stuffing
2 buttons for eyes, 18 mm (¾ in) in diameter

Cutting:
Make a set of patterns from the graph on page 44, following the line marked Monoclonius on the tail. This makes a toy 17·5 cm (7 in) tall and 38 cm (15 in) long. Cut a pair of all fabric body pieces and cut the frill lining and the horn from felt.

Fold each leg on the underbody gusset, so that it is easier to sew the curved dart at the inside top of the leg. Trim darts. Sew centre seam of underbody, leaving an opening between X and X for stuffing. Now sew the centre back seam of the side bodies. Position the underbody gusset in place and sew each side from the head backwards, towards the tail. Reinforce the corners at the top of each leg. Continue sewing back along the remaining undertail seam that is formed by the side bodies. Clip all corners and trim all seams made so far.

Finger press open the seam along a leg (see Figure 32, part 1), then pull leg fabric out on each side to form a sole. Sew across each point in turn, at right angles to the pressed seam. Cut the points and release any leg seams that have become trapped in making the sole (see Figure 32, part 2). Form the remaining three soles in the same way. The skin is now ready to be turned and stuffed. Start with the tail, then head, shoulders, buttocks, legs and body generally. Close the opening.

Make both the head frill and lining by sewing the centre seams of each between A and B. Place right sides of the head frill and the frill lining together, matching A to A and B to B. Sew the two together from A to B through E on each side. Clip angles, trim curves and turn right side out. Press.

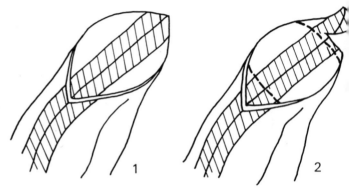

Figure 32 Preparation of sole for Monoclonius
1 Finger pressed leg seam   2 Corners stitched to form sole

Position the frill on the body and catch in place with a few stitches on either side.

Make the felt horn by sewing both pieces together along the two long edges. Turn the horn right side out and stuff very firmly. Place on front of the head and sew in place. Some people may find it easier to sew the horn to the frill before the latter is sewn to the head, especially if they don't have a curved needle. Sew on the button eyes, pulling them in tightly to form eye sockets. This will also help to anchor the frill to the body more securely. Additional stitching may be needed to hold the frill down along the mouth edge and across the shoulders, as for Protoceratops.

Triceratops

One of the dinosaurs well known to children the world over is Triceratops, which is immediately recognizable by the huge head with three horns and a neck frill. This armour must have been invaluable as protection against the large meat-eating dinosaurs like Tyrannosaurus, which lived at the same time. Both these dinosaurs died out about 65 million years ago.

Materials:
- 50 cm (½ yd) of 120 cm (48 in) wide fabric
- 30·5 cm (12 in) square of felt
- 396 g (14 oz) stuffing
- 6 pipe cleaners
- small piece of felt for eye background
- 2 buttons for eyes, 2·5 cm (1 in) in diameter

Cutting: Use the Monoclonius pattern graph on page 44 to make the body pattern for Triceratops. Follow the line marked Triceratops on the tail. Make the pattern for the head frill and horns from the graph. This makes a toy 17·5 cm (7 in) tall and 46 cm (18 in) long. The frill lining and horns are cut from felt, while the body is cut from fabric.

To make up the body, follow the instructions given for Monoclonius.

Place the right sides of the head frill together and sew the centre seam from A to B. Now sew the centre seam of the frill lining from A to C and D to B. Place right sides of the frill and the lining together and sew round entire outer edge. Clip into each scallop of the frill and trim any other tight curves. Turn completed head frill right side out and press the edges. The felt lining gives body to the frill and will help it to stand. If you use lightweight fabrics to make the head frill, then insert a layer of foam cut to shape. This will give the support required. Lay frill in position and hold with pins.

Sew both the long brow horns on the machine. Trim off the points and turn right side out. You must do this carefully. The horns are tightly stuffed and include a core of pipe cleaners. Take three pipe cleaners for each horn and bend into the correct length, which is slightly smaller than that of the horn. Place a little stuffing in the point of the horn first, then insert the pipe cleaners and continue stuffing. Sew the horns in position. Make the small nasal horn, turn, stuff and sew to the head.

Cut an eye background from the felt and put behind the button. Sew button into the eye position. Make second eye in the same way. Finish Triceratops by sewing the frill to the body at E, along the mouth line and across the shoulders.

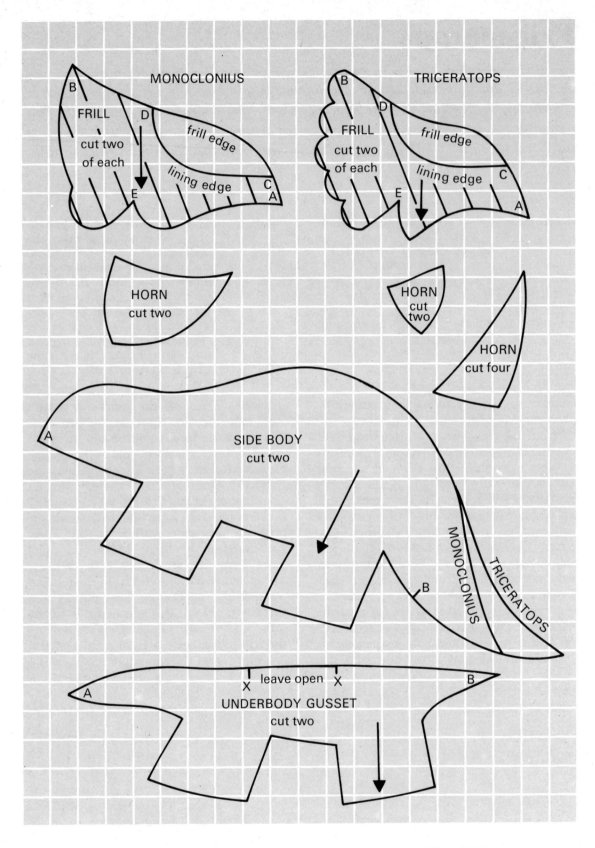

MONOCLONIUS

B

FRILL

cut two
of each

D

frill edge

E

lining edge

C
A

TRICERATOPS

B

FRILL

cut two
of each

D

frill edge

E

lining edge

C

A

HORN
cut two

HORN
cut
two

HORN
cut four

A

SIDE BODY
cut two

B

MONOCLONIUS

TRICERATOPS

X leave open X

A

B

UNDERBODY GUSSET
cut two

Pattern graph 8   Monoclonius and Triceratops *one square = 2·5 cm (1 in)*

6   The Giant Plant-Eaters

The largest dinosaurs known to us include such familiar names as Cetiosaurus, Bronto-saurus, Diplodocus and Brachiosaurus, the last being the biggest land animal ever known, weighing twenty times as much as an adult elephant. They were all sauropod dinosaurs, living in or near swamps and feeding on the vegetation. Most of them had very large bodies with thick legs, long slender necks with small heads, and elongated tails. The early relatives of these giants, like Yaleosaurus and Plateosaurus, were smaller animals, known as the prosauropods. They were intermediate to the giant plant-eaters on the one hand, and the large meat-eating dinosaurs like Tyrannosaurus on the other.

Yaleosaurus

Yaleosaurus was one of the earliest dinosaurs found in the fossil record and collected in North America. It was rather small, no more than 2·2 m (8 ft) long, having short limbs and a slightly elongated neck. Prosauropods walked on their hind legs but could also descend on to all fours. Plateosaurus was a larger related form found in Europe.

Materials:
30·5 cm (12 in) square of felt
60 cm (⅔ yd) of 120 cm (48 in) wide material
454 g (1 lb) stuffing
10 pipe cleaners
black, white and orange felt for eyes
embroidery thread for mouth

Cutting:
Make a set of patterns from the pattern graph. This will make a finished toy standing 34 cm (13½ in) high and 61 cm (24 in) long. Cut the hands, toes and soles from felt and all other body pieces from the fabric.

Sew a felt hand to each arm piece, matching A to A and B to B. Do be careful to keep the arms in pairs when doing this. Place two arm pieces together and sew on the wrong side. Leave the top of the arm open. Turn right side out and stuff to within 2·5 cm (1 in) of the opening. Now place the arm in the arm slot with the fingers pointing forwards and sew from C to D. Make second arm in the same way and attach to the side body.

Sew both side bodies together from the nose at E down the centre back to F. Insert body gusset, matching E to E, and baste in position. Check for evenness before sewing. Sew both sides in turn, checking that the arms are tucked out of the way and leaving a small opening on one side for turning. Make the opening low down so that a leg will hide it. Finish the underbody seam between the end of the gusset and F. Turn skin right side out and stuff. Close the opening.

Place a pair of leg pieces together with

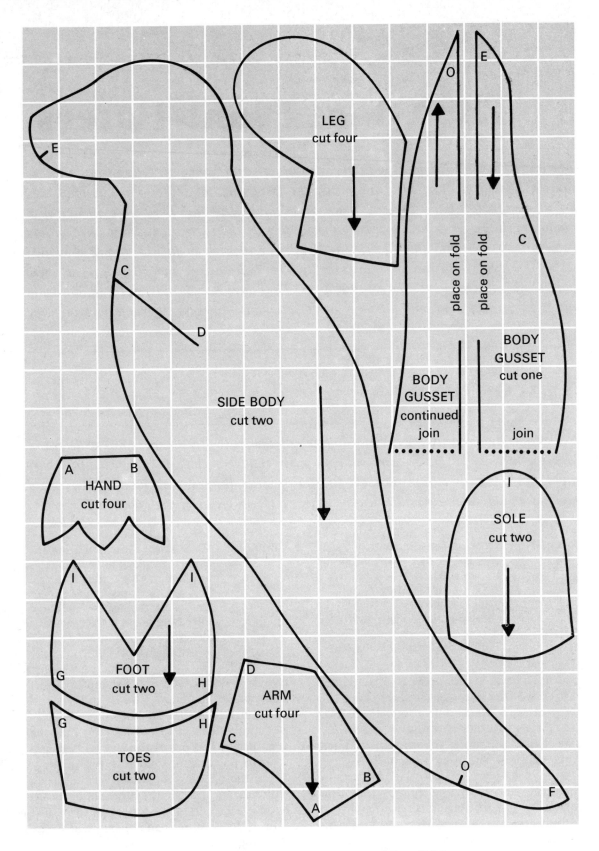

Pattern graph 9   Yaleosaurus *one square = 2·5 cm (1 in)*

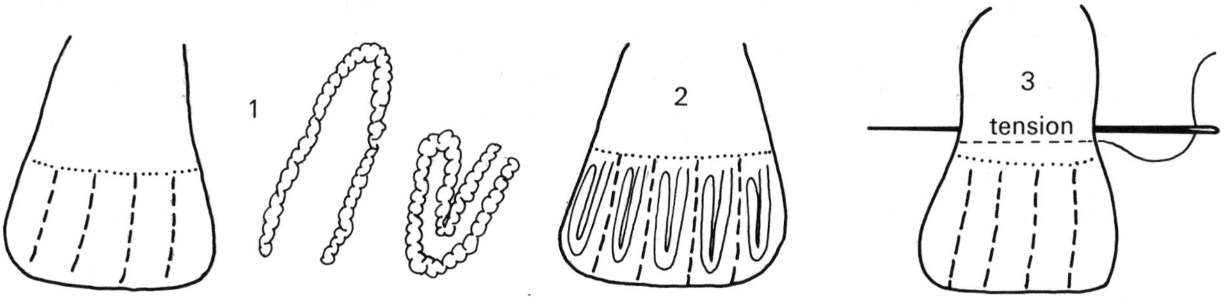

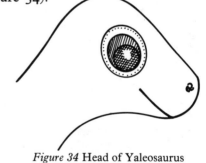

Figure 33 Construction of foot for Yaleosaurus
1 Top stitched toe channels and folded pipe cleaner   2 Pipe cleaners in channels   3 Needlemodelling behind
toes to shape foot

right sides facing and sew around the outer curved edge. Leave the base open. Turn right side out and stuff. Now sew a set of felt toes to a foot from G to H. Sew this completed upper foot to a felt sole from I, round the toes to I. Turn right side out and top stitch four rows across the felt to make five toe channels (see Figure 33, part 1). Take a pipe cleaner and fold it in half, twice. Slip the folded edge into a toe channel. Make the remaining four toes in the same way (see Figure 33, part 2). Carefully work tiny wisps of stuffing around each pipe cleaner to fill up the channels. Stuff the rest of the foot. Close the short seam starting at I, by hand, working back towards the central hole. Place the open end of the leg on top of the foot and ladder stitch the two together. Make the second leg in the same way.

The feet may appear very broad and, to a certain extent, you can minimize this by a little needlemodelling. Work a few stitches back and forth from G to H, pulling up the required amount (see Figure 33, part 3).

Now the legs can be sewn to the side of the body, in a variety of positions. One leg forward with the foot flat on the ground and the other leg back with the toes bent, gives Yaleosaurus a walking posture. With both legs together, he stands rather like a kangaroo. The tail can also be used to make a third point of contact with the ground, which gives increased balance. An upright posture makes a more suitable toy than one which is leaning forward. The position of the arm slots can also be altered to suit any of the leg positions.

Cut three circles of felt for the eyes. Use Figure 34 as a guide. Sew the black centre to the middle orange layer and sew this in turn to the eye white. Work a block of white stitches on the black felt as highlights before you sew the completed eye to the head. Make the second eye in the same way. Use the embroidery thread to make two nostrils and a chain stitched mouth (see Figure 34).

Figure 34 Head of Yaleosaurus

Brontosaurus

Scientists cannot agree whether the giant sauropods lived permanently in the lakes, where water helped to support their weight, or whether they only escaped to water from the hunting carnivores or to bathe. Brontosaurus, which means 'thunder lizard', is the most popular of all the dinosaurs. It lived in North America, while in Europe there was Cetiosaurus and in Africa, Brachiosaurus. Sadly, there is an earlier name for Brontosaurus which scientists now use. It is Apatosaurus.

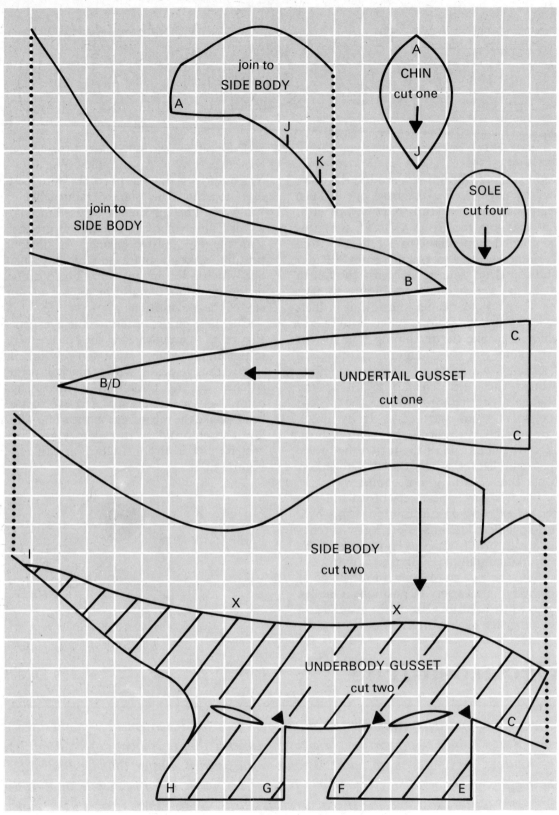

join to
SIDE BODY

A

CHIN
cut one

J

SOLE
cut four

A

J

K

join to
SIDE BODY

B

C

B/D

UNDERTAIL GUSSET
cut one

C

I

SIDE BODY
cut two

X

X

UNDERBODY GUSSET
cut two

C

H

G

F

E

Pattern graph 10   Brontosaurus *one square = 2·5 cm (1 in)*

The Armour-Plated Dinosaurs (*opposite*) *Left :* Ankylosaurus. *Right :* Stegosaurus.

Materials: 1 m (1 yd) of 120 cm (48 in) wide material
142 cm (56 in) wire
adhesive tape and binding for wires
1 kg (2 lb 4 oz) stuffing
black and white felt for eyes

Cutting: Make a set of patterns from the pattern graph, being careful to join the pieces together. This makes a toy 34 cm (13½ in) tall and 91 cm (36 in) long. Open out the fabric and cut in half, across the width, as described in Chapter 2. Cut all pieces from the fabric.

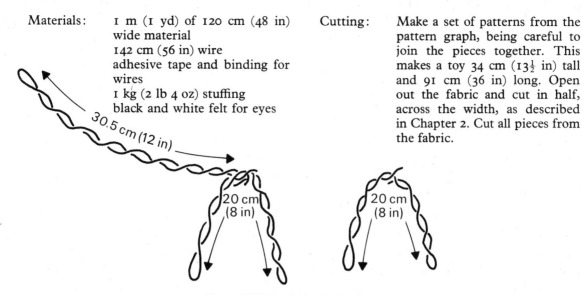

Figure 35 Skeletal wire for Brontosaurus

Commence making Brontosaurus by preparing the wire armature. Cut the wire into one 61 cm (24 in) and two 40·5 cm (16 in) lengths. Read the general instructions for wiring in Chapter 2 and then fold the wires according to Figure 35. This will make a neck and front leg bridge and a hind leg bridge. Tape, bind and cover the wires.

Make the buttock dart on each side body, then place them right sides together and sew the centre back seam from A to B. Place both underbody gusset pieces together and sew the centre seam on the wrong side. Leave an opening between X and X for turning and stuffing. Lay this gusset with right side uppermost and fold each leg in turn to sew the dart at the inside top of each leg. Now sew undertail gusset to underbody gusset, matching C to C on each side (see Figure 36).

Lay matching half of underbody and side body together with right sides facing and baste from D to E, F to G and H to I. Repeat on the other side and check for evenness before sewing. Insert soles. Trim

and clip all corners carefully.

Insert underchin gusset, matching A to A and J to J, and sew on each side, breaking the stitching at A so as not to trap the seam. Continue sewing back from J to K. Insert neck armature between K and I.

Prepare the skin for stuffing and then turn right side out. Stuff the head and tail first. Follow this by stuffing the base of each leg. Position the hind leg bridge and hold each arm of the bridge in place by ramming stuffing around the wires until they are well and truly embedded in the body. At no time should you be able to feel that the toy contains wires. Now insert the combined neck and front leg bridge and start by embedding the leg wires. Use the opening in the neck to embed the neck wire, and continue stuffing the rest of the body through the opening in the underside of the toy. Close openings with ladder stitch.

Using Figure 37 as a guide, cut two eye whites and two black pupils. Sew pupils to eyes and work a few white stitches on the pupils to make highlights before sewing the completed eyes to the head.

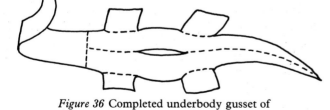

Figure 36 Completed underbody gusset of Brontosaurus

Figure 37 Construction of eye for Brontosaurus

Tyrannosaurus, Tyrant King of the Lizards (*opposite*)

7 Iguanodon and the Duck-Bills

These bird-hipped dinosaurs were all herbivores. They stood upright, walking on hind legs that had large, three-toed feet. These animals possessed so many bird-like features that some scientists have suggested that they are more closely related to birds than to other reptiles. Iguanodon is the most well-known European dinosaur, while the duck-bills occupy the same position in North America. Nevertheless, fossils of all these reptiles have been found scattered over the world, with a record of Iguanodon even inside the Arctic circle.

Kritosaurus

The webbed hands and feet of the duck-billed dinosaurs suggest that these reptiles swam. The front of the head was flattened into a broad toothless duck-like bill, while the teeth for grinding were located at the back of the mouth. More fascinating however, were the head crests which many duck-bills possessed. Some were solid, while others were hollow. Corythosaurus had a helmet-shaped crest, whilst that of Kritosaurus was scalloped.

Materials: 50 cm (½ yd) of 140 cm (54 in) wide fur fabric
46 × 30·5 cm (18 × 12 in) contrasting fur fabric
pair of 16 mm safety eyes
396 g (14 oz) stuffing

Cutting: Make a set of patterns from the pattern graph. When finished, Kritosaurus is 33 cm (13 in) tall and 38 cm (15 in) long. Cut all pieces from main coloured fur and the crest and soles from the contrasting colour.

With right sides together, sew the centre front seam from A, round the tail to B. Match A of crest to A of body and sew each side in turn from A to C. Fold crest in half at D, bringing both sides together, and sew from D to C. Clip the bottom of each scallop. Turn the skin right side out between B and C. Safety eyes are inserted at this stage.

Top stitch the crest along the four guide lines marked on the pattern. This makes five channels with a scalloped edge (see Figure 38). Now stuff the toy by starting with the tail, then each of the crest channels, followed by the head, neck and body proper. Close the opening. Place a pair of arm pieces together and sew round the edge, leaving an opening. Turn, stuff and

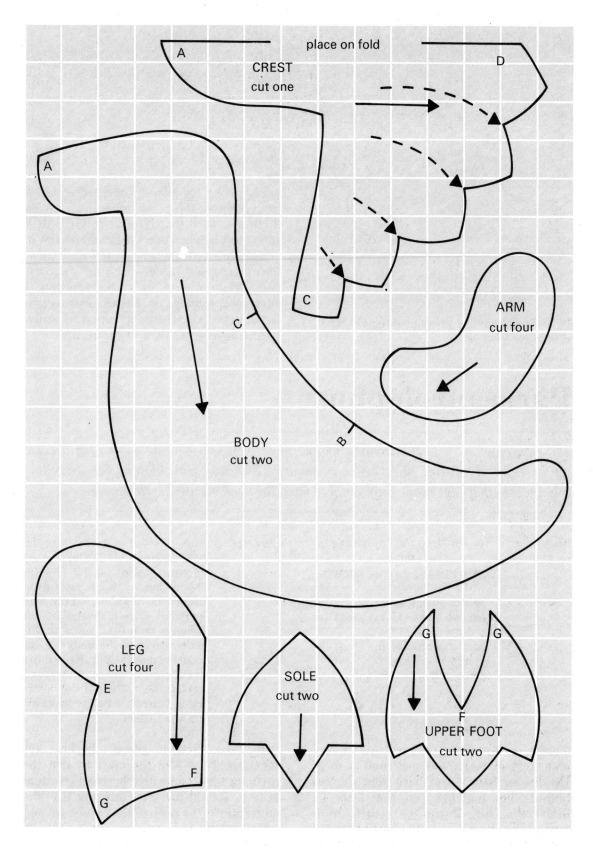

place on fold

A

CREST
cut one

D

A

C

C

ARM
cut four

B

BODY
cut two

LEG
cut four

E

F

G

SOLE
cut two

G   G

F
UPPER FOOT
cut two

Pattern graph 11   Kritosaurus *one square = 2·5 cm (1 in)*

Figure 38 Kritosaurus, showing formation of head crest by top stitching

close opening. Ladder stitch the arm to the body and make the second arm in the same way.

Place two leg pieces together and sew from F round top of leg down to E. Attach the upper foot, matching G to G, F to F and G to G. Sew. Insert the sole and sew in place. Turn leg right side out and stuff. Close the opening and ladder stitch the leg to the body. Make second leg in the same way. I have sewn the legs on Kritosaurus so that the toy is in a sitting position. Finally, release any fur trapped in the seams.

Parasaurolophus

Parasaurolophus had an elongated hollow head crest which could have been used as an air reservoir during underwater swimming. The beak was adapted for shovelling into the mouth scraps which were grubbed from the mud or pulled from plants.

Materials:
50 cm (½ yd) of 140 cm (54 in) wide fur fabric
38 × 30·5 (15 × 12 in) contrasting fur fabric
pair of 20 mm safety eyes
pair of 3 cm (1¼ in) joints for arms
pair of 4 cm (1¾ in) joints for legs
566 g (1 lb 4 oz) stuffing

Cutting:
Make a set of patterns from the pattern graph. This makes a toy 58·5 cm (23 in) tall by 58·5 cm (23 in) long. Cut the crest from the contrasting coloured fur. The toes and soles may also be cut from the same fur if you wish. All other pieces of the body are cut from the main colour. Remember to cut pairs where necessary, and to read the instructions on jointing in Chapter 2 before proceeding any further.

Commence by sewing the body. Match A of chin to A of body, and sew from A to B. Do this for both sides. Place right sides of both bodies together and sew from C, under the chin, down the centre front, around the tail and up to the opening in the centre back. Insert the crest, matching C to C at the front and D to D at the back on both sides. Sew in place, checking for evenness. Now fold the crest so that the two long edges come together, and sew from D to E. Refold the crest to bring E to the underside in the centre (see Figure 39) and sew across the top, shaping both corners by rounding them off. Turn the completed body right side out and insert the safety

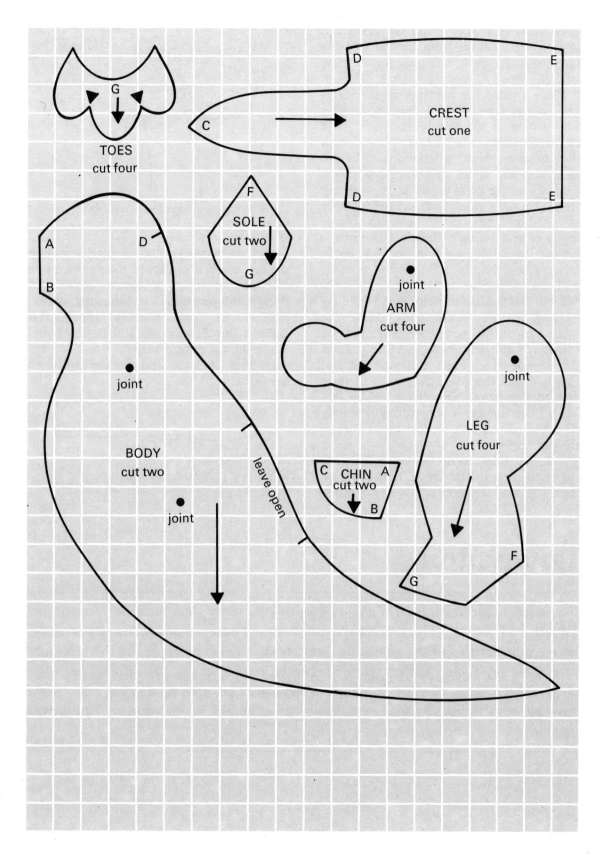

Pattern graph 12   Parasaurolophus *one square = 2·5 cm (1 in)*

eyes. Now turn skin inside out again and sew the short seam from D down to the opening in the back. Set aside for the time being.

Place a pair of arm pieces together and sew on the wrong side. Leave an opening for turning at the shoulders. Turn, stuff and work a joint into the arm before closing the shoulder. Make a second arm in the same way and check that you have a pair. Finish jointing arms to the body, working from the right side of an unstuffed body skin. Make the legs by placing a pair together and sewing each side, but remember to leave the base and the top open. Insert a sole, matching F to F and G to G, and sew. Clip the corners, turn leg right side out and stuff. Insert a joint and finish by jointing the leg to the body. Make the second leg in the same way. Take up two toe pieces and sew them together around the outside edge. Turn right side out and lightly stuff. Now place the toes to the foot and ladder stitch along both top and bottom edge, inserting any more stuffing that may be required. Make a second set of toes in the same way.

The last thing to do before stuffing the toy is to prepare the crest. This must be separated into an upper and lower channel.

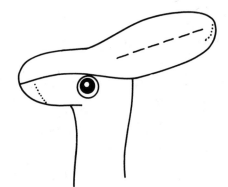

Figure 39 Construction of head crest for Parasaurolophus

Either machine a row of top stitching along the line marked in Figure 40 or work a row of stab stitching by hand. Now stuff Parasaurolophus in the following order: chin, lower crest channel, upper crest channel, head, neck, tail and central body. Close the opening. Finally, release any fur trapped in the seams and give the toy a good brushing.

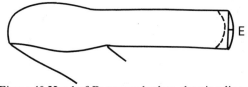

Figure 40 Head of Parasaurolophus showing line of top stitching

Iguanodon

Stories about the discovery of Iguanodon occupy a unique place in the history of fossil collecting. At first only the teeth were found, followed by large limb bones and eventually, twelve years later in 1834, a partially complete skeleton. It was only due to the persistence of the discoverer, Gideon Mantell, and his wife, that it was realized that these remains belonged to a giant herbivorous reptile. This was Iguanodon, the second dinosaur ever described, which can always be recognized by the characteristic spiked thumbs.

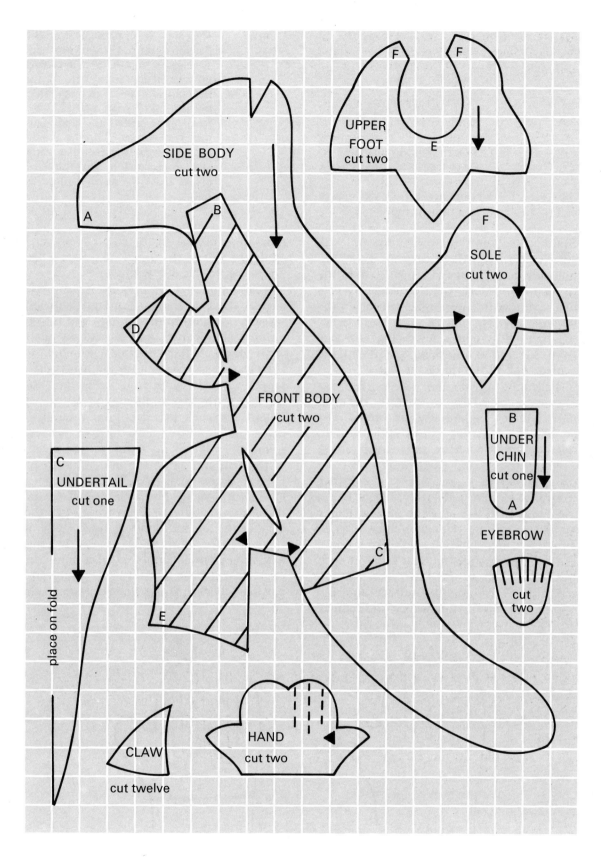

Pattern graph 13   Iguanodon *one square = 2·5 cm (1 in)*

Materials: 70 cm (¾ yd) of 120 cm (48 in) wide fabric
61 cm (24 in) of wide ric rac
908 g (2 lb) stuffing
4 pipe cleaners
23 × 61 cm (9 × 24 in) felt for hands and claws
2 buttons for eyes, approx 18 mm (¾ in) in diameter
7·5 × 15 cm (3 × 6 in) felt for eyebrows
embroidery thread for mouth and nostrils (optional)

Cutting: Prepare a set of patterns from the pattern graph. When finished, Iguanodon stands 48·5 cm (19 in) tall and 66 cm (26 in) long. From the fabric, cut a pair of side bodies and front bodies, two feet, one underchin and one undertail gusset. Cut the hands and claws for the toes from the large piece of felt, and the eyebrows from the smaller piece of felt.

Start by making the crown darts on both side body pieces, then baste the ric rac to one side body from the crown dart to the tip of the tail. Ease the ric rac gently into place, so that it is not under tension in the finished toy. Now place both side bodies together with right sides facing and sew from A, around the head and down the centre back to the tip of the tail.

Take a front body and fold the arm over to sew the curved dart at the top of the arm. Now fold the leg and sew the curved dart at the top of the leg. Trim both darts to release the tension. Make the corresponding darts on the second front body. The two front bodies may now be sewn together from B to C. Sew underchin to front body, matching B to B, and likewise sew under tail gusset to front body, matching C to C. This seam, across the base of the front body, is a good place to leave open for stuffing if you are an experienced toymaker. Simply sew 1 cm (½ in) on either side, leaving the middle by C open. If, however, you require more room to work in, then leave an opening along the side of the undertail gusset when you sew it to the side body.

The completed front body is now laid against the side body, with right and left sides in position. Match D to D and E to E on each side in turn and sew. Open out a wrist edge, lay a felt hand in place, matching D to D, and sew. Attach second hand in the same way to the wrist edge. Now open out the base of the legs and match upper feet at E and sew each in turn. Fold a hand to bring the thumb edges together, and sew round the edge of the hand, up the inside of the arm and along the underchin to A. Repeat on the other side. Working on each leg in turn, bring both back edges of the upper foot together and sew from F, up the back of the leg and down along the side of the tail. Insert a sole in the base of the foot, matching F to F, and sew all around the edge. Work over all seams, clipping and cutting before turning the skin right side out.

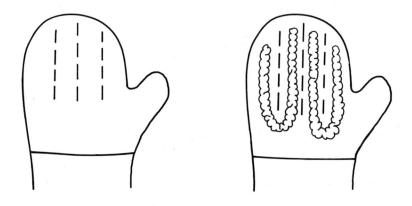

Figure 41 Finger construction for Iguanodon

56

The hands are formed around a pipe cleaner skeleton. This gives flexibility to the fingers, so that they can be bent into many different positions. Make channels for the pipe cleaners by top stitching three rows on each hand. Follow Figure 41 to get the position. Now take a pipe cleaner and fold it in half to make two fingers. The fingers will look much more lifelike if you bind them with knitting wool. It will also help to make a better fit in the channels. Bind sufficient wool over the length, then bend armature into a 'U'. Push the two arms so formed into a pair of adjoining channels in the hand. Push them home as far as possible, so that the tops are hard against the felt seam of the hand and the bend is at the base of the fingers (see Figure 41). Make the remaining three pipe cleaners into more fingers for the rest of the hands. Hold all the fingers in place by pushing small pieces of stuffing around the base of the pipe cleaners and even up into the fingers if necessary. Stuff the thumb, hand and arm on each side.

The skin of Iguanodon is rather complex to stuff, because the shape is awkward to get at comfortably. However, patience, careful routine and constant turning and checking for evenness will ensure a pleasing result. You have already stuffed the hands and arms, so now work on the feet and legs of both sides respectively, followed by the tail. Leave sufficient room just inside the tail so that you can still get your hand inside the toy to stuff the head and body. Pack out the cheeks and crown before making a firm neck. Finish stuffing the toy by working on the chest and body proper, then the top of the tail, just inside the opening.

Check that Iguanodon stands comfortably and looks smooth on all sides. Close the opening and remove any excess stuffing from the surface of the toy.

The feet will appear a little unbalanced until they have the claws added to the toes.

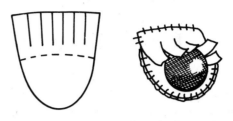

Figure 42 Construction of eye for Iguanodon

Take a pair of felt claws and sew the two long sides together on the right side. Stuff very firmly and then position on a toe and hand sew in place. Work five more claws in the same way.

It only remains now to add the finishing touches to the face: the eyes, mouth and nostrils. Sew a button to the lower part of the felt eyebrow. You may have to build up the back as outlined in Chapter 3 if you use a button with a shank. Fold the lashes over the top of the button and catch in place on the fold with very tiny stitches. Position the completed eye on the side of the head and buttonhole stitch round the curved edge and hem across the top fold (see Figure 42). Work another eye in the same way. Decide whether your Iguanodon needs a mouth or nostrils. This will depend on the pattern of your fabric and whether you want to use the mouth to give further character to the toy. Use embroidery thread to work a chain stitch mouth, and a small block of satin stitches to make the nostrils.

8 The Armour-Plated Dinosaurs

Some of the plant-eating dinosaurs were covered with an amazing array of plates, spines, spikes and tough leathery skins. These probably acted as protection and defence against the hunting predators. Although these were all bird-hipped dinosaurs, they were divided into two separate groups known as stegosaurs and ankylosaurs.

Stegosaurus

The fossil remains of many different stegosaurs have been found all over the world, but the dinosaur known as Stegosaurus lived only in North America. It was about 8 m (25 ft) long, stood on four legs and had a very small head. Along the back and standing upright was a double row of enormous plates, and on the end of the tail were two pairs of long spikes.

Materials: 1·7 m (1⅔ yd) of 120 cm (48 in) wide fabric
122 × 38 cm (48 × 15 in) foam sheeting, 1 cm (½ in) thick
1·25 kg (2 lb 12 oz) stuffing
23 cm (9 in) square of felt
small piece of felt for eye backing
2 buttons for eyes, 2·5 cm (1 in) in diameter

Cutting: Make a set of patterns from the pattern graph. Stegosaurus measures 81 cm (32 in) long and 40·5 cm (16 in) tall. You will have to open out the fabric to full width in order to cut the body, remembering to cut left and right sides where necessary. There are four sizes of plates, two of each size for each side of the body. Each plate has a pair of pieces, so you will cut a total of thirty-two fabric plate pieces. Cut sixteen foam plate linings, using the plate patterns less the seam allowance. Cut the spikes from the felt square.

Prepare all the plates first by placing pairs together and sewing round the edge, leaving the straight edge open. Turn right side out and insert a foam lining. Now baste the open edges together to hold the foam in place and prevent slipping when you sew the plates to the body. Put aside a pair of small plates for the head and divide the remainder into two equal sets. Take one set and baste them to the body from A to B (see Figure 43). Arrange the second set of plates on the other side of the body in such a way that they will be staggered with the first set. The body gusset can now be inserted between the two body sides. Baste this first before sewing, and check that all

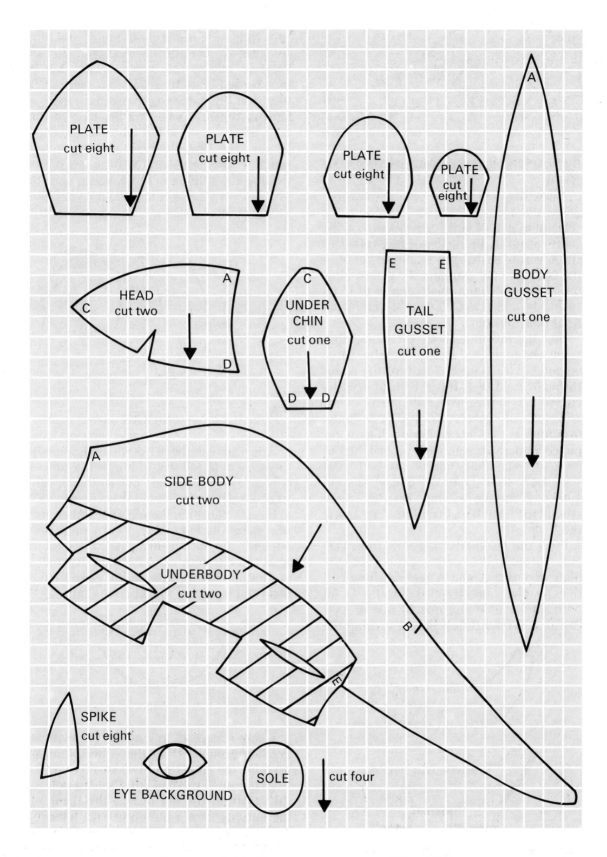

PLATE
cut eight

PLATE
cut eight

PLATE
cut eight

PLATE
cut eight

BODY
GUSSET
cut one

A

HEAD
cut two

A

C

D

UNDER
CHIN
cut one

C

D   D

TAIL
GUSSET
cut one

E   E

SIDE BODY
cut two

A

UNDERBODY
cut two

B

E

SPIKE
cut eight

EYE BACKGROUND

SOLE   cut four

Pattern graph 14   Stegosaurus *one square = 2·5 cm (1 in)*

59

Figure 43 Stegosaurus, showing position of the plates

the plates are safely caught in their respective seams.

Make the head by first sewing the cheek darts on each side piece. Position the remaining pair of small plates and sew the centre seam, A to C. Leave just sufficient space at A to enable you to join the head to the body without trapping the plates. Now insert the underchin, matching D to D on each side, and C to C. Turn the completed head right side out.

Sew the two underbody pieces together along the mid line, leaving a rather large opening. This is needed to turn the plates through. Fold each leg in turn to sew the curved dart at the top (see Figure 44). Now sew the tail gusset to the underbody, matching E to E on each side. The completed underbody can now be matched to each corresponding side of the body and sewn back from D to the end of the tail gusset. Continue sewing the tail seam around the tip to B on the upper side. Insert the four soles.

Push the head, which is now right side out, through the neck opening of the body. See that A and A are matching and that no plates are trapped. D and D on both sides should also match. Sew around the neck several times. Before turning the

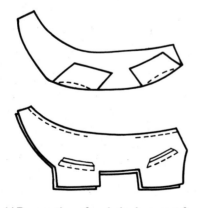

Figure 44 Preparation of underbody gusset for Stegosaurus

skin right side out trim all seams and clip the corners. Do not forget to trim the leg darts to release the tension. The skin is now ready for stuffing. Cut four foam soles to put in the base of each leg. This gives a smooth finish as well as a flat base to the feet. Stuff the head and tail first, followed by the legs, then the body proper. Stegosaurus is best left standing for a few hours to allow the stuffing to settle. When you are satisfied that the skin is firm enough, close the opening.

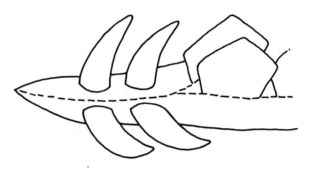

Figure 45 Position of tail spikes on Stegosaurus

The weight of the plates will undoubtedly cause them to fall over. However, a row of ladder stitch worked down the inside edge of each row will hold them up proud.

Place a pair of spike pieces together and sew along the long edges. Turn right side out and stuff very firmly. Make three more spikes in the same way. Position the spikes in pairs on either side of the centre back seam and hand sew in place (see Figure 45).

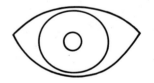

Figure 46 Felt eye shapes for Stegosaurus

Using Figure 46 as a guide, cut two felt eye backgrounds from the same colour as used for the spikes and two smaller circles from the small piece of felt. Punch a hole in the centre of the felt to take the shank of the buttons. Sew a button to each felt eye, building up the back as described in Chapter 3. Glue and stitch the eyes to each side of the head.

60

Ankylosaurus

Ankylosaurus was an armoured dinosaur living about 65 to 100 million years ago. Like other ankylosaurs, the body was somewhat flattened and very heavy, so that the animal walked on all fours. The back was covered with bony plates and a row of spines projected from each side of the body. The tail ended in a swollen bony lump which was probably able to swing from side to side as a weapon.

Materials: 60 cm (⅔ yd) of 120 cm (48 in) wide fabric
340 g (12 oz) stuffing
46 cm (18 in) square of felt
2 knobbly buttons for eyes
embroidery thread for stitchery

Cutting: Prepare a set of patterns from the pattern graph. When finished, Ankylosaurus measures 51 cm (20 in) long by 17·5 cm (7 in) tall. Cut the body pieces from a textured fabric that is suggestive of armour plates. If you cut the top and bottom parts of the body on the fold make sure that you iron out the creases. The spines are cut from felt. There are three different sizes; cut two pairs of 1, two pairs of 2 and fourteen of 3.

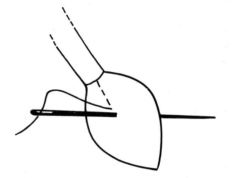

Figure 47 Needlemodelling on the tail lump of Ankylosaurus

Sew the upper body to one side body, matching A to A and B to B. Sew the second side body to the other side of the upper body, again matching A to A and B to B. Be careful to sew the correct seam allowance at the neck, otherwise the head may well be lopsided. Now insert the under-body between the two side bodies, matching C to C and D to D on each side, and sew. Leave an opening on one side for turning. Finish the body by sewing across the mouth from A/C to A/C.

Turn the skin right side out and stuff. Mould the body carefully so that there are cheeks, neck, body proper and tail. The end of the tail has been left open, as you will sew the tail lump on to it. Sew around the curved edge of the tail lump, leaving the straight edge open. Turn right side out and stuff. Fold under the straight edge, push the lump on to the end of the tail and ladder stitch the two together. Using a long needle, work tiny stitches down the centre of the lump to needlemodel a groove between the two sides (see Figure 47). If you have used a textured fabric to make the toy, these stitches will be invisible. Close the stuffing opening in the side of the body when you are satisfied with the shape.

The four legs are all made in the same way. Take a pair of legs and sew the front edge from E to F. Open out the ankle edge of the leg, match an upper foot, F to F and G to G, and sew. Close the foot and leg together and sew the back leg seam from H through G to I. Insert the sole, matching H to H, and sew all round the edge. Turn the completed leg right side out and stuff through the hip opening. When you have made all four legs, arrange them in pairs on either side of the body, so that the feet and tail lump are on the ground while the rest of the body is raised. Ladder stitch the legs to the side body, leaving

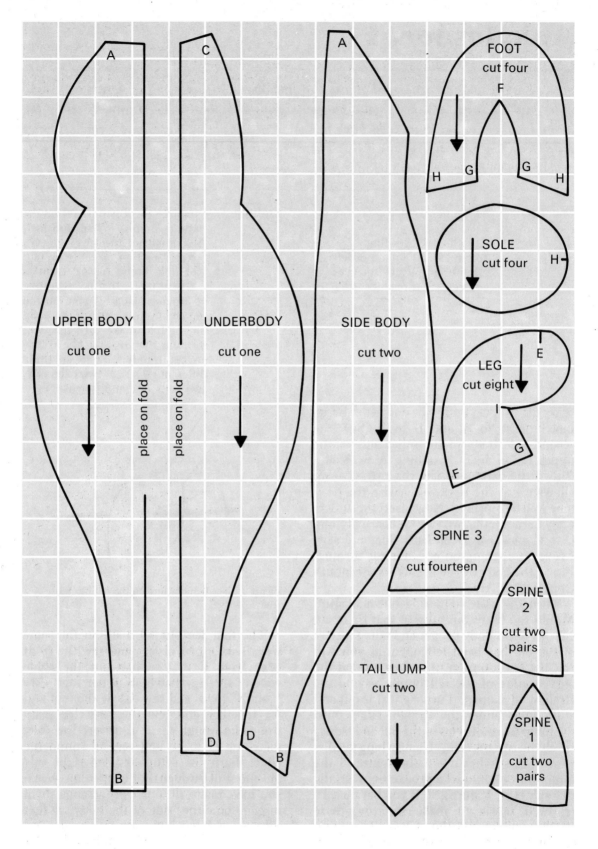

A

C

A

FOOT
cut four
F

H   G   G   H

SOLE
cut four   H

E
LEG
cut eight
I
F   G

UPPER BODY

cut one

place on fold

place on fold

UNDERBODY

cut one

SIDE BODY

cut two

SPINE 3

cut fourteen

SPINE
2
cut two
pairs

TAIL LUMP
cut two

SPINE
1
cut two
pairs

D

D

B

D

B

B

Pattern graph 15   Ankylosaurus *one square = 2·5 cm (1 in)*

62

Figure 48 Position of spines and legs on Ankylosaurus

space above to sew on the spines (see Figure 48).

Make all the spines first, then sew them to the sides of the body in one operation. The two large spines have two side seams. Place felt together in pairs and sew the two long edges. Turn right side out and stuff firmly. The fourteen smaller spines have only one side seam each. Fold so that the straight edges come together, then sew.

Again turn right side out and stuff. Now sew the spines to the side of the body, following Figure 48 as a guide.

Sew the buttons to either side of the head to make eyes. If the toy is for a very young child then substitute felt eyes, which are safer.

Ankylosaurus is now ready for the finishing touches. Different fabrics need to be treated in different ways, so you must decide for yourself what your toy needs. The feet are rather elephantine in shape, so stitch claw marks with embroidery thread to give more shaping. A mouth can also be chain stitched in matching thread. If you use a plain fabric to make Ankylosaurus, design some plates to cover the back.

9 Tyrannosaurus, Tyrant King of the Lizards

Tyrannosaurus rex was the largest meat-eating animal that has ever lived, standing 5 m (16 ft) tall, 13 m (40 ft) long and weighing about 7 tons. It must have been a fearsome sight when running, being propelled by large hind legs ending in massive clawed feet, and the whole balanced by a thick muscular tail. Set above this was the large head with formidable jaws bearing an awesome array of teeth. Tyrannosaurus was the king hunter, using the clawed feet and jaws to hold and tear up the prey. The use of the small arms is a puzzle: they were too short to reach the mouth, and yet ended in two strongly-clawed fingers. Little wonder that this dinosaur was called Tyrant King of the Lizards.

Materials:
- 1·7 m (1⅔ yd) of 120 cm (48 in) wide fabric
- 1·5 kg (3 lb 4 oz) stuffing
- 38 cm (15 in) square of felt for claws
- 254 cm (100 in) wire for foot armature
- tape for binding wires
- 15 cm (6 in) square of foam sheeting, 1 cm (½ in) thick
- black, green and yellow felt for eyes
- 30·5 × 15 cm (12 × 6 in) white felt
- 30·5 × 7·5 cm (12 × 3 in) mouth lining fabric

Cutting: Make a set of patterns from the pattern graph. Join pieces where necessary and remember to open out folds. This makes a toy 56 cm (22 in) tall and 83·5 cm (33 in) long. Open the fabric out to full width and cut in half across the width. Place the two pieces together with any fabric pattern running in the same direction, and right sides together. Lay pattern pieces on the fabric, cutting pairs where necessary. In all, there will be twenty-six main fabric pieces. Cut the claws from felt – there are twenty of these. Cut two 30·5 cm (12 in) bias strips, each 3·5 cm (1½ in) wide from the fabric. These will be used to make the lips. Cut teeth and eyes from the various coloured felts (see illustration facing page 49). Make sure that you have read the instructions on wiring in Chapter 2.

Place the two body gusset pieces together with right sides facing and sew the centre seam from A to B. Match an inside leg to the body gusset and sew from C to D.

Repeat with second inside leg on the other side and then sew the small darts on each inside leg. Join the tail gusset to the base of the body gusset, but leave an opening in

Fliers and Gliders (*opposite*) *Top*: Pteranodon. *Bottom*: Rhamphorhynchus.

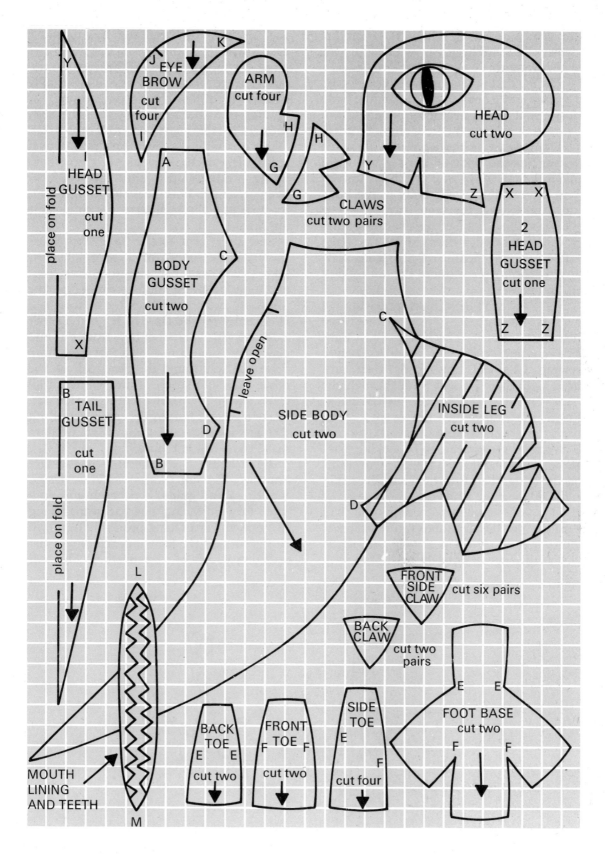

Pattern graph 16   Tyrannosaurus *one square = 2·5 cm (1 in)*

A Galaxy of Reptiles (*opposite*)
Top left : Dimetrodon. *Top right :* Lizard. *Centre left :* Stripey Lizard. *Centre right :* Deinosuchus.
Bottom : Ichthyosaurus. See back of wrapper for Gila Monster.

the centre on either side of B. There are two openings in this toy by which it may be stuffed, and this is the smaller of the two.

Sew the dart in the leg on each side body. Now lay a side body to corresponding body gusset and sew from the neck edge down the chest and along the front edge of the leg. Leave the base of the leg open. Continue sewing up the back of the leg and then along the tail to the end of the tail gusset. Join the remaining side body to the body gusset in exactly the same way. Now sew the centre back seam of the two side bodies from the neck edge down to the tip of the tail. Leave an opening in this seam. Sew any remaining seam under the tail beyond the tail gusset.

Make the head next. Start by sewing the neck darts on each head piece, then baste the head gusset between each side. Turn right side out and check for evenness before sewing. Clip and trim seams, then turn head right side out and push through the neck opening of the completed body. Position centrally, then sew in place. The head can also be placed off centre, so that Tyrannosaurus appears to be looking sideways, over a shoulder. Trim and clip seams on the body, then turn the completed skin right side out for stuffing.

This is a large toy to stuff and will consequently take time and require patience. There are two openings to work through as well as the open ends of the legs. Start with

the tail, then the head and legs. I find it easier to do this if the toy is supported over a large cardboard carton. The carton supports the extremities and also allows you to mould the toy without compressing the stuffing on either side. Now stuff the body proper, ie. the chest and abdomen areas. Work methodically and turn the skin over constantly to check evenness. Leave both filling positions open until the feet have been attached. This gives the stuffing time to settle and allows any cavities to become apparent.

Sew a felt claw to the tip of each toe – there will be sixteen of these in all. Now take a foot base, two side toes, one front and one back toe, and assemble in the following order: sew back toe to foot base from E round the claw to E on the other side; sew side toe to foot base from F round claw to E; sew front toe to foot base from F on one side round the claw to F on the other side, and so on. Trim points off all claws and then turn the foot right side out. Make a second foot in the same way. Both feet are identical, so there is no need to make right and left sides.

To make the foot armature, cut the wire into two 127 cm (50 in) lengths. Using Figure 49 as a guide, bend each wire into three forward facing, one backward facing and one upward facing prongs. These will be the toe and the leg supports. Now twist each double arm of wire together. This will

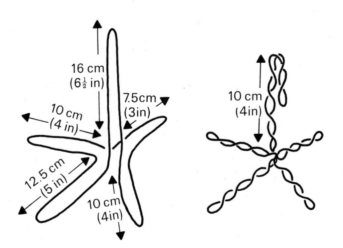

Figure 49 A leg and foot wire for Tyrannosaurus showing length of each part and how they should be twisted together

shorten the length but at the same time give more strength to the armature. Bend the top of the leg prong down against the main shaft so that the finished length is approximately 10 cm (4 in). Cover the wires as described in Chapter 2.

Place a small amount of stuffing into the point of each claw so that the wires will rest against this rather than the felt. Now slide the forward facing prongs in first and then the prong for the back toe. You may have to bend the armature slightly in order to accomplish this. Carefully work stuffing into each toe, around the armature, until the foot is fully stuffed. Ladder stitch the short seams between each toe, working towards the leg prong. The excess material can be gathered around the base of the leg prong, where it will be safely out of sight. Make the second foot in the same way. Since they are both identical they can be attached to either leg. Make sure that the legs are fully stuffed and turn under the seam allowance on the raw edge.

Make a central channel for the leg prong by pushing your thumb into the stuffing and gently working it back and forth until the space so made is able to accommodate the wire. Position the foot correctly, with three forward facing toes, then work several rows of ladder stitch between the foot and the base of the leg. The first row of stitching will act as basting, while you will be able to pull the stitches tighter on the second round. A third round should be worked with a separate thread for maximum effect. Attach the second foot in the same way, inserting any last little wisps of stuffing that may be needed.

Sew the felt claws to each arm from G to H, remembering to make pairs. Place one pair of arm pieces together with right sides facing and sew round the edge, leaving an opening at the shoulder. Sew a deep cleft between the claws, reinforcing the stitching on the turn, then slash between the claws

down as far as the fabric. This will make the two fingers which are so characteristic of Tyrannosaurus. Trim the point off the claws, turn right side out, and stuff. Close the opening with ladder stitch, then sew the arm to the body. Make the second arm in the same way and likewise ladder stitch it to the body. By sewing the arms to the body in this way, you will be able to control their positioning.

Place two fabric eyebrow pieces together with right sides facing and sew from I to J to K. Trim the curve and turn right side out. Cut a piece of foam to the shape of the eyebrow and insert between the fabric. Turn under the raw edge between I and K and ladder stitch the opening, then place the eyebrow on the head and hold in place with pins for the time being. The felt eye pieces may be either glued or stitched together. Decide which you prefer, then attach the black pupil to the green eye and these to the yellow eye background. Position the eye under the eyebrow and bring the sides of the eyebrow in close to the eye, so that it curves over it rather than lying flat on it, masking the eye. Make the eyebrow and eye for the other side before you finally decide on the position. Attach the eyes first, then ladder stitch the eyebrow in place.

Sew the felt teeth to the edge of the mouth lining so that you make an upper and a lower row. Now baste a bias strip along the bottom edge between L and M, and check that it is even before sewing. Lay the second bias strip along the top edge between L and M and check again before sewing. Turn both bias strips over to the back of the mouth piece, being careful to form neat corners at L and M. These bias strips form the upper and lower lips. If you want them more prominent, insert a piping cord in the bias turn. Place the mouth equally on either side of the head, then ladder stitch in place.

10 Fliers and Gliders

Flying reptiles – the pterosaurs – were a very familiar part of the dinosaur scene, although they themselves were not dinosaurs. The wing was formed by a web of skin supported by a greatly extended finger, the rest of the arm, the side of the body and the leg. It was more like the wing of a bat than that of a bird. Two very different groups of pterosaurs existed, and patterns for one of each are given here to make mobile toys. These will be particularly appealing to little boys, who will no doubt want to hang them from the bedroom ceiling.

Rhamphorhynchus

This little pterosaur lived in Europe and Africa about 140 million years ago. The pattern makes a nearly life-size toy as in reality Rhamphorhynchus had a wing span of only 76 cm (30 in). The elongated tail was flattened at the tip into a rudder which was probably used to control direction of flight.

Materials:
50 cm (½ yd) of 120 cm (48 in) wide fabric
106·5 cm (42 in) wire
adhesive tape for wires
170 g (6 oz) stuffing
6 pipe cleaners
30·5 cm (12 in) square of felt
small pieces of felt for eyes
3 eyes from hook and eye units
nylon fishing line and brass ring

Cutting:
Prepare a set of patterns from the pattern graph. Notice that the top and bottom pieces are obtained from one pattern that differs only in the mid line. The top is cut on a fold while the lower body has a tummy allowance. This makes a toy that has a wing span and length of 61 cm (24 in). Cut toes and fingers from felt.

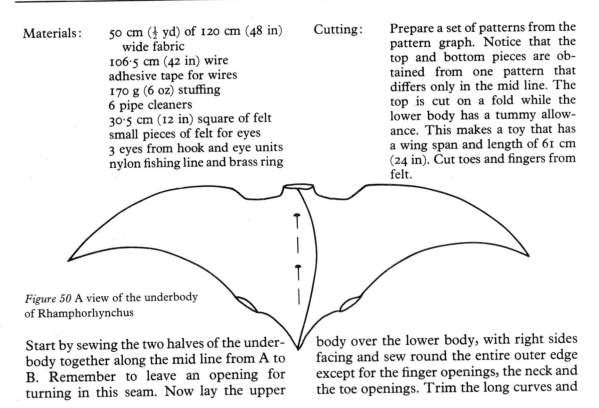

Figure 50 A view of the underbody of Rhamphorhynchus

Start by sewing the two halves of the underbody together along the mid line from A to B. Remember to leave an opening for turning in this seam. Now lay the upper body over the lower body, with right sides facing and sew round the entire outer edge except for the finger openings, the neck and the toe openings. Trim the long curves and

68

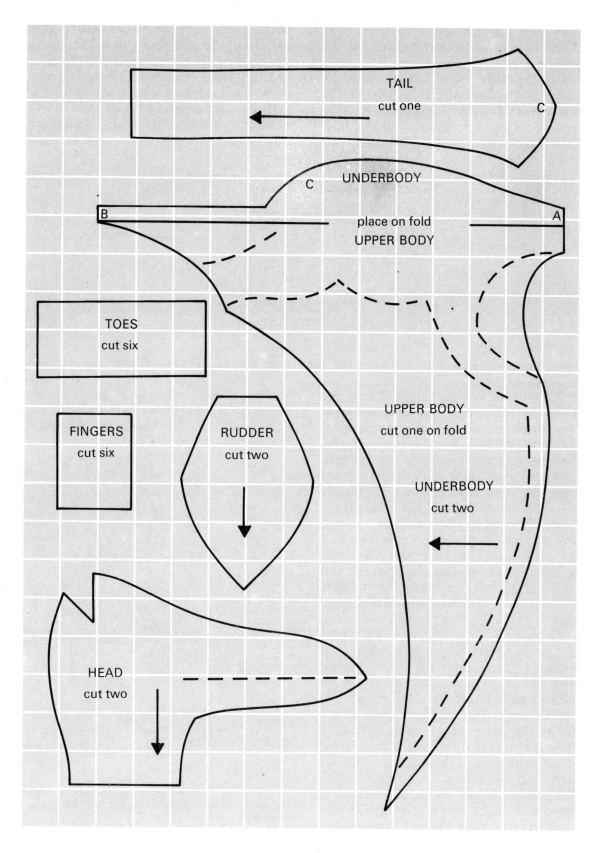

Pattern graph 17   Rhamphorhynchus *one square = 2·5 cm (1 in)*

69

then turn the completed skin right side out. Finger press or carefully iron flat the wing edges.

Lay the body flat on a table with the underbody uppermost. Now smooth the two layers of material together, working from the wing tips towards the mid line. Collect the excess material into a ridge and hold this flap with a row of pins (see Figure 50). Turn the skin over and either lightly pencil or tailor tack the outline of the arms and legs on to the fabric. Top stitch over these lines, working on each side of the mid line separately, folding the excess material of the underbody to the opposite side so it is not caught by the machine foot.

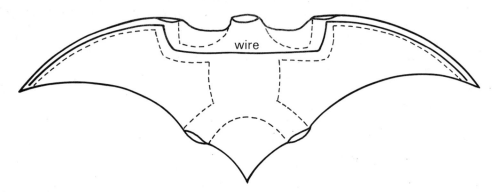

Figure 51 Rhamphorhynchus with top stitched body outline and skeletal wire in position

Cut a 76 cm (30 in) length of wire and bind the two ends with adhesive tape. Now thread the wire in through the opening on the tummy. Remove the pins from the ridge and feed an end of wire up each arm and down along the channel formed along the front edge of the wing. Gently bend the wire to fit the shape so that it lies easily in the fabric. Work stuffing into each arm through the finger openings then stuff the body proper and the legs. Close the opening on the centre tummy seam and also gather up the neck opening to close it. Leave the finger and toe openings open (see Figure 51).

To make a set of fingers, take a pipe cleaner and bend it into three fingers (see Figure 52). Lay three felt fingers on the table and cover upper surface of each with a layer of glue. Leave for a few minutes to become tacky. Now take each piece of felt in turn and fold it over a pipe cleaner finger. Make sure that all three folds lie in the same plane (see Figure 52) and that the edges of each piece of felt are firmly stuck down. When dry, cut the excess felt away and shape each finger into a pointed claw tip. Bend the two outer fingers in towards the middle finger, then slip the completed unit into the finger opening on the front edge of the wing. Sew securely in place before bending the fingers towards the wing tip for a more realistic effect. Make the second set of fingers in the same way.

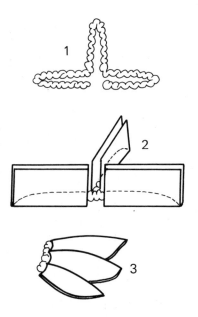

Figure 52 Method of constructing fingers for Rhamphorhynchus
1 Folded pipe cleaner   2 Felt shapes glued over each finger   3 Excess felt trimmed away to shape the fingers

70

To make the toes you need to take the remaining four pipe cleaners and fold each one in half. Lay the felt toes in a row on the table in front of you and again spread a layer of glue over the upper surface of each piece of felt. Leave to become tacky, then lay a folded pipe cleaner in the centre of each piece of felt. Fold the edges of the felt together and press really firmly to make sure that the pipe cleaners are stuck in place (see Figure 53). Trim the excess felt away with scissors, shaping each end into a claw. Fold each completed toe in half so that it in fact becomes two toes. Place four toes in each leg opening and sew securely in place. Bend toes slightly to lose the stiff effect.

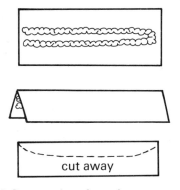

Figure 53 Construction of toes for Rhamphorhynchus. The final shaping is achieved by cutting away the excess felt

Fold the tail in half, lengthways, and sew down the long edge. Trim seam and turn right side out. Bind both ends of the remaining 30·5 cm (12 in) length of wire then thread it through the tail. Very carefully insert small wisps of stuffing into the tail till it both fills the tail and masks the wire. Now ladder stitch the broad end of the tail to the tummy, matching C to C. Work the ladder stitching down each side of the tail, catching it to the part of the wing that lies between the legs. Place both rudder pieces together with right sides facing and sew around the edge leaving the short straight edge open. Turn right side out. Feed the end of the tail through the rudder opening for a length of about 5 cm (2 in). Sew rudder to the tail and also work a few, very tiny stab stitches down each side of the tail to hold the rudder close to it (see Figure 54).

Make the darts in both head pieces then fold them right sides out and top stitch the mouth line on each side respectively (see Figure 55). Now sew the two head pieces together round the edge, leaving only the neck open. Turn right side out and stuff. Gather up the neck opening and fasten off. Position the head on the neck of the body and ladder stitch in place. Glue or stitch eye pieces together then sew on either side of the face.

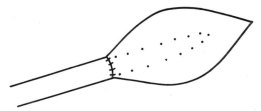

Figure 54 Position of stab stitches for finishing the rudder of Rhamphorhynchus

To mount Rhamphorhynchus as a mobile, sew the eye half of a hook and eye unit on to the upper side of each elbow and between the legs in the mid line. Nylon fishing line is used to string up the mobiles and as it cannot be tied with ordinary thumb or reef knots, you must learn the knots that anglers use. The two used here are the half blood knot and the double overhand loop knot (see Figure 56). The longer the length of line that you use, the greater the swing the mobile will have. However you must avoid hanging them so low that children will bump into them. Attach a length of line to each eye with a half blood knot then collect all the lines together on a brass ring, again using half blood knots.

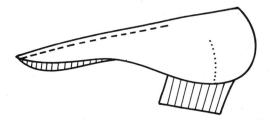

Figure 55 Method of top stitching the mouth for Rhamphorhynchus

Finish Rhamphorhynchus by bending the tail and wings upwards to give a pleasing line, and a sense of movement.

71

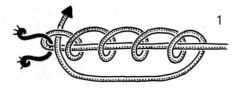

Figure 56 Knots to be used with nylon line
1 Half Blood Knot. Thread end of line, marked by arrow, through eye then wind back over line at least four times. Finally, take end of line and pass through loop next to the eye, pulling up firmly to close the knot   2 Double Overhand Loop Knot. Useful for making a secure loop at end of a line

Pteranodon

The second group of pterosaurs, the pterodactyls, lived about 80 million years ago. Pteranodon was the largest of all the pterosaurs, having a wing span of nearly 8 m (25 ft) and was also probably the largest creature that ever flew. It had no teeth and very little tail, while the back of the head carried an enormous crest.

Materials:
30 cm (⅓ yd) of 120 cm (48 in) wide fabric
112 cm (44 in) wire
approx 76 cm (30 in) adhesive tape for wire
112 g (4 oz) stuffing
15 cm (6 in) square of felt
46 cm (18 in) square of felt
4 pipe cleaners
small pieces of felt for eyes
2 eyes from hook and eye units
nylon fishing line

Cutting:
Prepare a set of patterns from the pattern graph. This makes a toy 66 cm (26 in) wide and 30·5 cm (12 in) long. Cut fingernails from the small square of felt and the fingers, toes and head crest from the large square. Pteranodon and Rhamphorhynchus are made very much the same way, so you will find it useful to refer to the illustrations of the latter.

Sew both underside pieces of the body together along the centre seam. Leave an opening for turning. Lay the upper body against the underbody and sew all around the edge, leaving the neck, finger and toe openings open. Sew between the legs to make the very short tail. Now turn the completed skin right side out and gently finger press the edges of the two wings. Cut away the points at the tip of both wings. These openings will be used later to take the wire armature. Now lay the completed skin flat on a table with the body top side up. Mark the outline of the body on to the fabric with a soft pencil or tailor's tacks. The outline is marked on the pattern. The excess material on the underside can be

collected together safely by following the procedure outlined for Rhamphorhynchus. When you have finished the marking, lay the skin under the machine foot and top stitch the outline.

Cut the wire into two 56 cm (22 in) lengths. A length will be used to make the armature for each wing. First bind the cut ends with adhesive tape, then bend the wire into the shape given in Figure 57. Each finger loop of wire must be twisted along its length. Bind each twist with adhesive tape. Now insert the long end of the wire into the finger opening on the front edge of the wing and gently feed it down the channel which has been formed by the top stitching. The end of the wire

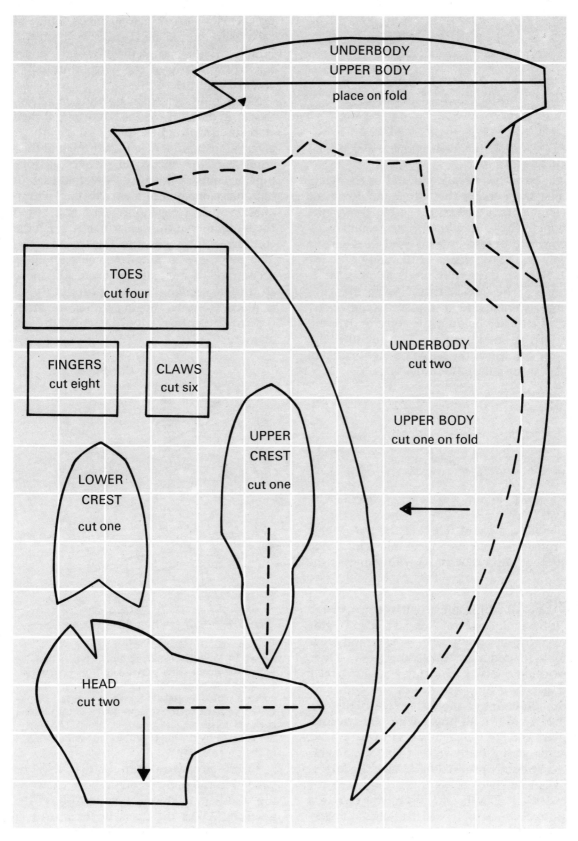

UNDERBODY
UPPER BODY
place on fold

TOES
cut four

FINGERS
cut eight

CLAWS
cut six

UNDERBODY
cut two

UPPER BODY
cut one on fold

UPPER
CREST

cut one

LOWER
CREST

cut one

HEAD
cut two

Pattern graph 18   Pteranodon *one square = 2·5 cm (1 in)*

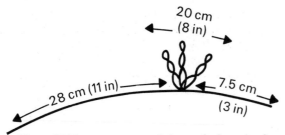

Figure 57 Measurements and shape of wing wire for Pteranodon

will pass through the cut end of the wing. The short end of the wire is fed down the channel that makes the arm. Leave the finger wires projecting. The second wing wire is prepared and inserted in the same way on the other side of the body.

Now very carefully insert wisps of stuffing into the arms so that it masks the wires and also holds them in place. Remove any pins that are holding the tummy flap and stuff the body proper. Close the opening. This still leaves the neck and legs open and also around the base of the fingers.

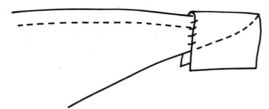

Figure 58 Construction of the wing tip finger for Pteranodon

Fold a piece of felt over the wire which protrudes from the tip of the wing. Stab stitch it into a claw and sew the edges to the wing. Trim away the excess felt (see Figure 58).

Lay all of the fingernail squares of felt on the table in a row. Spread a layer of glue over the upper surface of each and leave for a few minutes to become tacky. Then, working one at a time, lay a square over a finger wire and fold the edges together on the underside of the finger (see Figure 59, part 1). When all finger wires are covered, press the felt on each one in turn to make sure that it is really stuck, then leave fingers to dry before proceeding. Shape the fingernails into sharp claws by cutting away the excess felt. Now lay the contrasting coloured square of finger felt over the finished fingernail and stab stitch it along the underside (see Figure 59, part 3) trimming away the

excess felt again. When all three fingers of each hand are finished in this way you will be able to ladder stitch the base of the finger felt to the fabric of the wing, thus safely enclosing all the wires.

Lay a pipe cleaner along the centre of a foot strip of felt. Fold the felt over and then stab stitch close to the pipe cleaner. Shape each end to a point (see Figure 60) and then trim away the excess felt. Cover all four pipe cleaners in this way. Now fold each in half, place one pair of toes so formed within another pair (see Figure 60), and stitch them together at the base as a unit. Push the completed four toes into the leg opening. You may have to remove some stuffing to accommodate the toes or even add more stuffing to wedge them in securely. Stitch in place, securely, tugging at them to check the stitching. Insert toes in remaining leg opening.

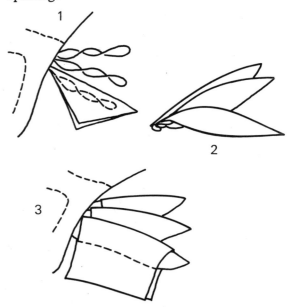

Figure 59 Method of making fingers for Pteranodon 1 Twisted finger wires protruding from opening in front edge of wing. One finger has already been covered with a diagonally folded felt square   2 All fingers covered by felt squares which in turn have been cut to shape, making the claws   3 The claw felt covered by the finger felt, leaving only the tip of the claw exposed

Insert any extra stuffing that may be needed in the body through the neck opening. Gather up the neck and close off the opening. Make the darts in the crown of both head pieces. Fold each side in half with right sides out and top stitch the line that

74

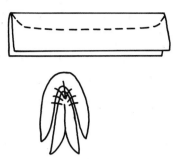

Figure 60 Construction of toes for Pteranodon

marks the mouth. Now place both head pieces together with right sides facing and sew the edge, leaving the neck open. Turn right side out and stuff firmly, taking extra care with the jaws. Close the neck opening.

The crest is made from two pieces of felt. Fold the upper crest to make the ridge and then top stitch the ridge, as close to the fold as you can manage. Place the lower crest to the upper crest piece and sew the two together around the outside edge. Do this on the right side of the felt and possibly use a contrasting Sylko for more effect. Place a little stuffing in the crest then sew it on the top, back part of the head. Look at the illustrations and the photograph facing page 64 to see the position. Each eye consists of three circles of felt. Stick or stitch these together and then to the head. Figure 61 shows the eye attached by a double cross stitch.

Sew the head to the body, placing neck gatherings over each other so that they are hidden. Pteranodon is strung as a mobile by sewing an eye from a hook and eye unit to each elbow on the upper side of the body. Attach a length of nylon line to each eye by a half blood knot. If a length of about 2 m (6 ft) is used, then tie each end to an eye and make a double overhand loop in the centre of the line (see Figure 56, page 72). This loop can then be placed over a hook in the ceiling or sewn to the bottom of a lamp-shade. When Pteranodon is hung up, bend the fingers and toes so that a gliding posture is adopted. The wings will splay out horizontally, unlike those of Rhamphorhynchus which can be bent into any position (see Figure 62).

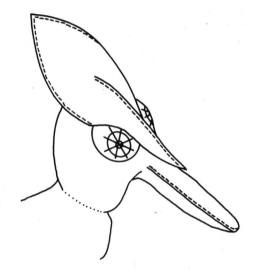

Figure 61 Head of Pteranodon showing position of mouth, eyes and crest

Figure 62 Pteranodon strung as a mobile

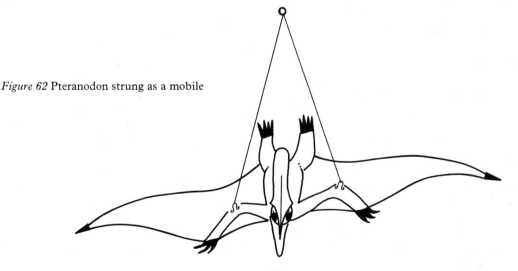

11 A Galaxy of Reptiles

During the Age of Reptiles there was a wide variety of different life forms inhabiting the land, air and sea. Yet only a few reptiles are found living today, for now, mammals and birds must be considered supreme. This galaxy of toys includes a few from the past and the present.

Deinosuchus

Since crocodiles made their appearance about 130 million years ago Deinosuchus has been the largest. It measured 12 to 15 m (40 to 50 ft) long and probably lived in swamps preying upon large dinosaurs that came to drink.

Materials: 30·5 cm (12 in) square of wadding
30·5 cm (12 in) square of fabric for underbody
25 cm (¼ yd) of 140 cm (54 in) wide fur fabric
1·8 kg (4 lb) rice or alternative filling
15 cm (6 in) square of felt
small pieces of yellow and black felt for eyes

Cutting: Make a set of patterns from the pattern graph. This makes a toy that is 46 cm (18 in) long. Cut a pair each of side bodies and side heads, two eyelids and one only chin from the fur fabric. Cut two underbody pieces, one from fabric and one from wadding. The eyes are cut from felt.

Lay wadding to the wrong side of the underbody and sew round the outer edge to mask the rice filling in the toy. Place both side bodies together and sew the centre back seam from A to the tip of the tail. Now lay underbody between side bodies and sew from B to C on both sides. Finish undertail seam from C to the tip. Clip all corners, especially between the toes.

Sew the dart on each side head then place them right sides together and sew the top seam from A, forward to the snout. Insert chin and sew on both sides from B, forward to the snout. Turn head right side out and insert in the neck opening of the body, matching A to A and each B to B. Sew A to B on each side, leaving B to B on underside open. Turn completed skin right side out

and fill the toy with rice. Leave sufficient slack so that the toy is able to move and assume different postures. Close opening securely.

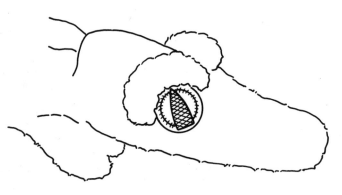

Figure 63 Completed eye of Deinosuchus

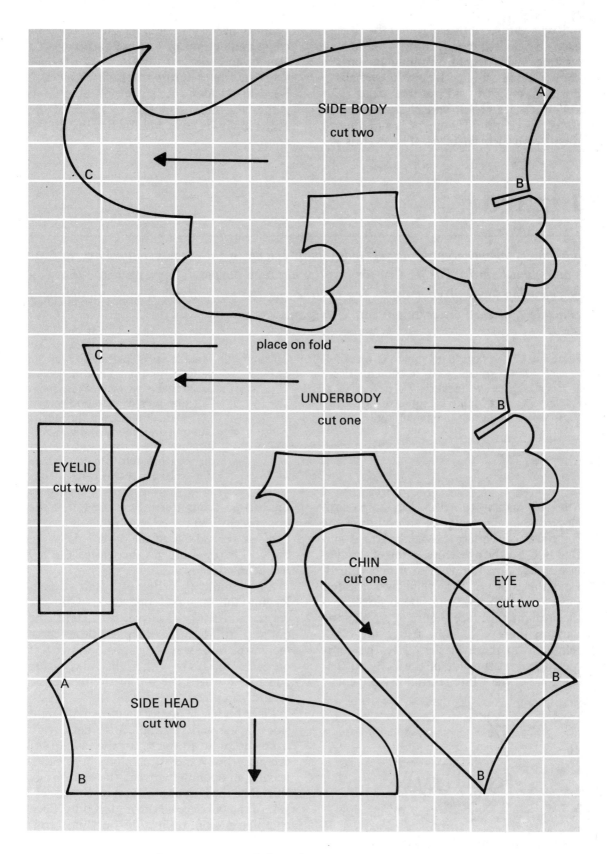

Pattern graph 19   Deinosuchus *one square = 2·5 cm (1 in)*

Run a gathering thread round the edge of each circle of white felt. Insert a knobble of stuffing in each before pulling up on the thread and fastening off. Sew the eyeballs in position on each side of the head. Cut yellow circles of felt and black felt pupils for each eye using Figure 63 as a guide and then neatly hem in place. The eyelids are simply made by folding under the raw edges and hemming. Lay each strip over an eyeball and ladder stitch in place on both short sides and across the back of the eye. By using ladder stitch you will be able to gather the fullness across the back of the eye. Finally, release any fur trapped in the seams.

Lizard

The most common reptiles living today both belong to the same group. They are the snakes and lizards. The pattern for this toy has been purposely kept simple so that you can develop ideas of your own. Try lengthening the tail, adding a crest, designing a chameleon or even converting it into a dragon.

Materials:
15 cm (6 in) square of black felt
50 cm (½ yd) of 120 cm (48 in) wide fabric
15 cm (6 in) square of white felt
340 g (12 oz) stuffing

Cutting: Make a set of patterns from the pattern graph. This makes a lizard that is 58·5 cm (23 in) long. Cut one pair of side bodies and four pairs of feet from the fabric. Cut one underbody and two eyelids from the fabric and the eye pieces from felt. Do not fringe the eyelashes at this time.

Start by making the eyes. Lay an eyelash along the straight edge of an eyelid on the right side of the fabric. Match A to A and B to B. Place the eye white on top of the eyelashes, again matching A to A and B to B. Fold the edges of the eyelid over the felt pieces and then sew from side to side across the straight edge (see Figure 64). Make the dart on the eyelid. Now fringe the black felt to form the eyelashes. Lay the completed eye on the side of the body so that the edge of the white felt follows the curve

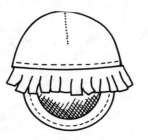

Figure 64 Lizard, showing relationship of eyelashes, eyelid and eye

marked on the pattern. Sew the felt to the body as close to the edge as possible. Make and sew second eye to the other side of the body. The eyes are finished after the toy has been stuffed.

Sew around the edge of a pair of feet, leaving the straight edge open. Clip the corner and trim the curve, turn right side out and stuff lightly. Make the other three feet in the same way. Now position two feet on each side body with right sides facing and toes towards the top of the toy. Baste securely in place.

Place both side bodies together with right sides facing and sew the centre back seam from the snout to the tip of the tail. Insert the underbody and stitch along both sides, leaving an opening between the legs on one side. Sew the remaining seam on the underside of the tail beyond the underbody. Turn completed skin right side out and stuff, first the tail, then the head and lastly the body proper. Close opening.

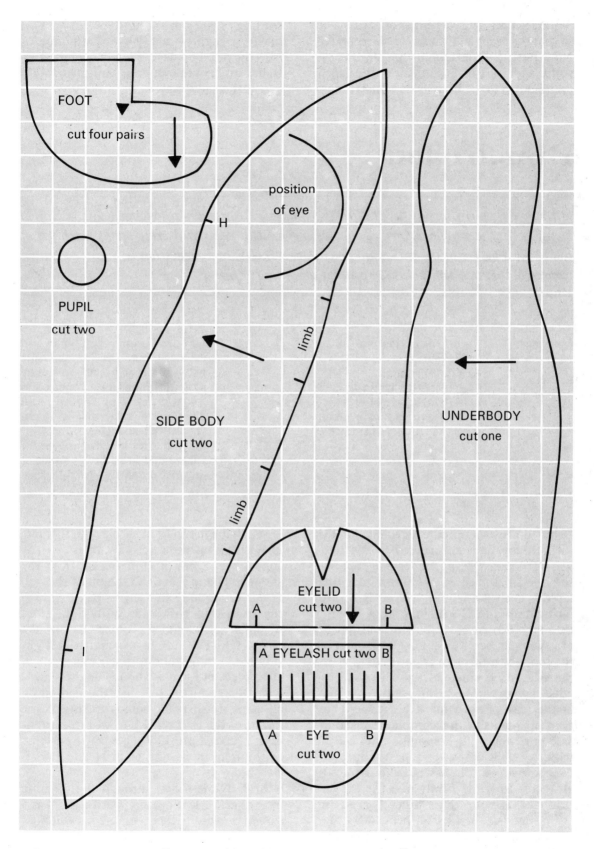

FOOT
cut four pairs

PUPIL
cut two

H

position
of eye

limb

SIDE BODY
cut two

limb

I

UNDERBODY
cut one

EYELID
cut two

A   B

A EYELASH cut two B

A   EYE   B
cut two

Pattern graph 20   Lizard *one square = 2·5 cm (1 in)*

Finger press the raw edges of each eyelid so that the seam allowance is turned under. Now push a little stuffing under the eye white and start to ladder stitch the fabric eyelid down to the body fabric. Insert more stuffing as you work around the curve. This makes a slightly raised eye. Now glue or hem the pupil in place. Finally trim the eyelashes if they are too long. Finish the other eye in the same way.

Dimetrodon

Although frequently considered with the dinosaurs this animal belonged to the Sailed Lizards that were characterized by the enormously expanded crest along the back of the body. The use of the sail is unknown, nevertheless one suggestion is that it was used to control the body temperature by either absorbing or losing heat.

Materials:
1 m (1 yd) of 120 cm (48 in) wide fabric
454 g (1 lb) stuffing
15 cm (6 in) square of white felt
15 cm (6 in) square of black felt
38 × 25·5 cm (15 × 10 in) foam sheeting, 1 cm ($\frac{1}{2}$ in) thick

Cutting: Use the pattern graph for Lizard to make patterns for the side body, underbody and eyes. The pattern graph for Dimetrodon has the new feet and the sail. This makes a toy that is 33 cm (13 in) tall and 58·5 cm (23 in) long. Cut the toy as outlined for Lizard and in addition, a pair of sail pieces and two pairs of legs.

Read the instructions for making Lizard, as both toys are constructed in the same way. To make a complete leg and foot first sew the small dart on the upper foot then lay this against a leg piece with right sides facing and C to C matching. Sew from D through C to E. Now fold leg and foot so that you can sew the side seam from F at the top, down through D and E to G at the bottom. Insert sole and sew all round the edge, taking care to reinforce the stitching at the base of each toe. Clip corners and trim off points. Turn completed leg right side out. Following the guide lines on the pattern, work a row of top stitching between each toe. There will be four rows in all. Stuff each toe firmly and the leg less firmly. Make the three other legs in the same way and then baste them to the side of the body so that the leg seams are lying on the inside.

Work the first part of each eye so that it is in position on the side body then sew the centre back seam of Dimetrodon from the snout to H and from I to the tip of the tail. Insert underbody and sew in place. Finish the seam under the tail. With right sides together sew round the outer edge of sail from H to I. Trim curves and turn right side out. Using the sail pattern as a guide, cut a piece of foam to slip inside the sail. It will need about 1 cm ($\frac{1}{2}$ in) trimmed off on all sides. Push foam points up into fabric points of the sail. Work a row of top stitching to each point. Lay sail against one side of the body matching H to H and I to I. Sew securely in place.

Stuff Dimetrodon through the opening in the back. Close opening between sail and side body with ladder stitch. This will hold the foam upright. Finish the toy as described for Lizard.

St George and the Dragon (*opposite*)
Top: Dragon and St George. *Bottom:* Princess and King.

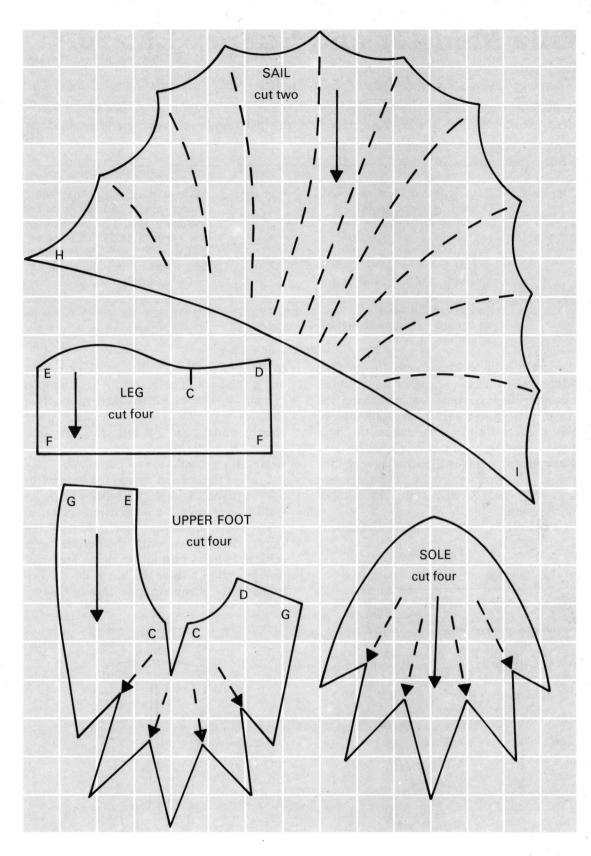

SAIL
cut two

H

LEG
cut four

E C D

F F

G E

UPPER FOOT
cut four

C D

C G

SOLE
cut four

I

Pattern graph 21   Dimetrodon *one square* = *2·5 cm (1 in)*

The Dragon (*opposite*)

Gila Monster and Stripey Lizard

The conspicuous colouration of the Gila Monster makes it easily recognizable. This is perhaps a fortunate coincidence as the lizard has a poisonous bite. It lives in desert areas of the southern states of the USA. A fun version of this reptile can be made by using all your colourful remnants of wool.

Materials:
- 4 50 g (2 oz) balls of double knitting (thick) wool
- 23 cm (9 in) square of salmon felt
- 15 cm (6 in) square of reddish satin
- small piece of foam sheeting to line tongue
- 340 g (12 oz) stuffing
- 23 cm (9 in) square of black felt
- 2 buttons for eyes

Cutting: Make a pattern for the mouth lining, tongue and feet from the pattern graph. The finished toy has a length of 68·5 cm (27 in). Cut mouth linings from salmon felt, tongue from satin and the feet from black felt.

Choose suitably coloured wool for the Gila Monster, namely a dark brown and an orange-yellow contrast for crocheting the 'tiger' patterning on the body. Rather more than half of the wool should be the dark brown. Use a No. 3·5 ISR crochet hook to work the toy – this is slightly larger than is frequently used for wool of this thickness and will consequently result in a more pliable skin.

The Gila Monster is worked throughout in double crochet with a scalloped crest along the back. The pattern is very simple, relying on shapes rather than number of stitches or rows and for this reason is more clearly understood by following the diagrams. It would also be a good toy to use for teaching a child to crochet.

Start at the tail end by making a chain for 6·5 cm (2½ in), and work a block of crochet until it measures the proportions given in Figure 65. The background colour of the skin is dark brown while the patterning is achieved by working random areas of orange-yellow to give the 'tiger' effect. Try to avoid too many straight lines of colour.

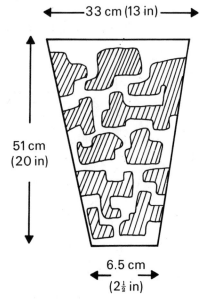

Figure 65 Guide for making body of Gila Monster

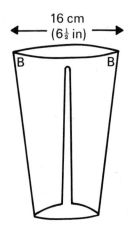

Figure 66 Shaping of the neck for Gila Monster

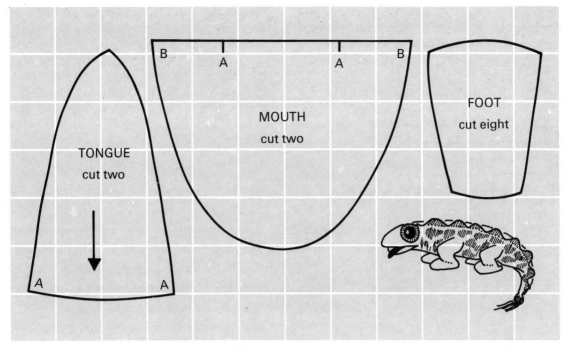

When you have the correct length, join the two sides with a slip stitch and work three complete rows, as in Figure 66. Continue crochet in dark brown to make the head. Lay the skin on the table with the edges uppermost so that you can mark the corners of the mouth. Now using Figure 67 as a guide, work an upper and a lower head. These will simply be two equal sized flaps.

Place a mouth lining against the right side of the upper head and sew around the outer curved edge. Any irregularities on the edge of the crochet will of course be lost in the machining of the lining. Work the lower mouth lining in the same way. Now place the two tongue pieces right sides together and sew around the outside edge. Turn right side out and insert a foam sheet filling which has been cut to size. Position the tongue on the straight edge of the mouth lining, matching each A to A and sew the inner lining edge from B through A to B on the other side.

With the completed skin right side out work a scalloped crest down the centre back seam. Join the two sides together at the same time and also stuff the toy as you work towards the tail. Any combination of stitches can be used to make the scallop as it is only an effect that you are after.

Each leg consists of a crocheted rectangle measuring 10 × 12·5 cm (4 × 5 in). Sew the two long sides together to make a tube. Stuff the leg and sew one end in place on the side of the body. Now take up an upper and lower felt foot and sew around the outside edge on the right side. Insert a knobble of stuffing through the opening in the ankle, then sew the foot to the base of the leg. Work remaining three legs in the same way.

Crochet two orange circles for the eye

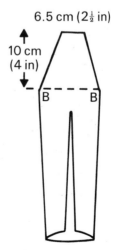

6.5 cm (2½ in)

10 cm (4 in)

Figure 67 Shaping of the head for Gila Monster, with relevant measurements

83

backing. They should be just slightly larger than the buttons. Sew a button to the centre of each circle, then sew the completed eye units in place on either side of the head. If the mouth gapes too wide, you might like to sew the upper and lower jaw together for a short distance from each corner.

Make a tassel from all the remaining wool and finish the Gila Monster by sewing this to the end of the body as a tail. Now bend the toy backwards and forwards to evenly spread the stuffing.

Stripey Lizard is made in the same way but has simple felt shapes for the eyes. Choose a main body colour, say green, and use this for the tail, head and legs. The rest of the toy may be crocheted in stripes, using all your colourful remnants.

Ichthyosaurus

The children's jingle 'She sells sea shells on the sea shore' commemorates Mary Anning, who collected fossils along the sea coast of southern England during the early part of the nineteenth century. Many of these fossils were sold from her shop and to museums all over the world. Amongst the many fossils she discovered were the remains of the first complete skeleton of Ichthyosaurus. This was a marine reptile having the appearance of a present-day dolphin.

Materials:
50 cm (½ yd) of 120 cm (48 in) wide fabric
30·5 cm (12 in) square of felt
340 g (12 oz) stuffing
30·5 cm (12 in) square of foam sheeting, 1 cm (½ in) thick
15 cm (6 in) square of white felt
15 cm (6 in) square of dark blue lurex
2 buttons, 2·5 cm (1 in) in diameter

Cutting:
Make a set of patterns from the pattern graph. The toy is 58·5 cm (23 in) long and 30·5 cm (12 in) tall. Cut main body pieces from the fabric, limb linings from the large square of felt and the eyes from white felt and lurex. Remember to reverse the pattern when cutting pairs of any piece.

Make the four limbs first by sewing a fabric and felt piece around the outside edge. Turn right side out and lightly stuff to within 2·5 cm (1 in) of the open end. Hold stuffing away from the opening with large tacking threads or pins so that it can be basted to the side body. Arrange limbs in pairs so that the large pair is in front while the smaller pair is at the back.

With right sides together, sew the two pieces of the top fin together around the outer curved edge. Trim the curves and turn right side out. Cut a piece of foam sheeting to insert in the fin. Now baste the fin to one side of the body matching A to A and B to B.

Machine each white felt eye background to a side of the body. Work a series of criss cross rows over the felt so that they form a nine point star. The centre of this stitching will be covered by the lurex eye leaving only the points exposed. Use contrasting coloured thread for this stitching to add more interest to the eye. Run a gathering thread around the edge of a lurex circle and partly draw up. Insert a knobble of stuffing then a button. Finish drawing up on the gathering thread and fasten off. The button gives a good outline to the rim of the eye. Now sew the lurex eye to the middle of the eye background. Work a second eye in the same way.

With right sides together, sew both side bodies together from C around the tail to D on the underside. Insert the underbody and sew along both sides from C to D

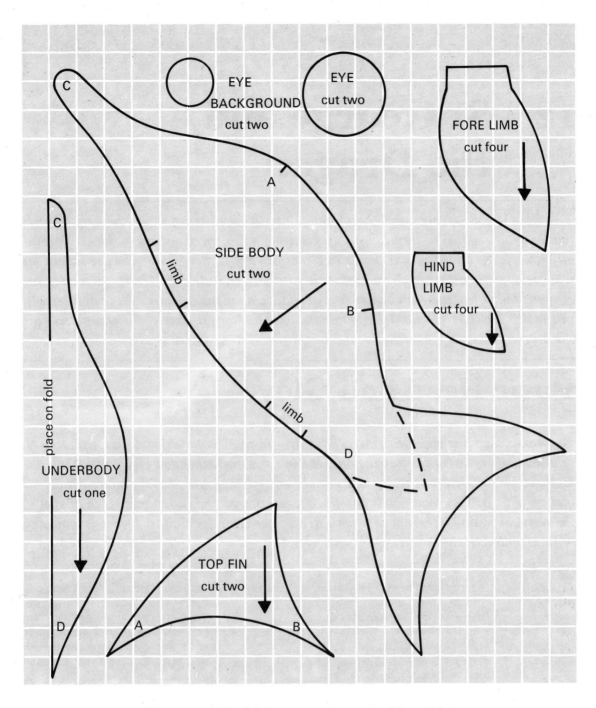

Pattern graph 23   Ichthyosaurus *one square = 2·5 cm (1 in)*

leaving a small opening on one side between the limbs. Trim and clip seams before turning right side out. Cut a piece of foam sheeting to insert in the two lobes of the tail fin. Hold this in place by top stitching the line marked on the pattern. Now stuff Ichthyosaurus firmly, starting with the tail and snout and working back to the body proper. Close the opening with ladder stitch.

12 St George and the Dragon

The legend of St George and the Dragon dates back to the time of the Crusades. It relates to a Kingdom terrorized by a dragon who preyed on the young maidens. Eventually, the King's daughter was chosen as a sacrifice and although loved by her family she was abandoned on the sea shore to meet her fate. Fortunately St George, a wandering Knight, found her there and after a great battle he managed to slay the dragon. All this makes a wonderful plot for a puppet play. The story is simple, the characters few, the dragon fearsome and of course there is plenty of action with the battle.

Basic Head and Glove

St George, the King and the Princess have their heads and gloves made in the same way, so instead of repeating the instructions several times over, they are given here. Only the features are different as these relate to the character being made. Therefore details for making the eyes, hair and hands are given together with the clothing for each puppet in the relevant section. It would be as well to read the complete chapter before making any of these characters.

Materials (head):
- sheet of cardboard or cylinder from a toilet roll
- flesh-coloured nylon stocking or leg of tights
- 112 g (4 oz) stuffing
- 4 m (4 yd) any scrap wool
- foam block such as a bath sponge
- 25·5 cm (10 in) by 17·5 cm (7 in) long piece of stockinette
- strong linen thread

(glove and hands):
- 50 cm (½ yd) of 90 cm (36 in) wide fabric
- sheet of cardboard or cylinder from a toilet roll
- 23 cm (9 in) square of flesh-coloured felt
- 8 pipe cleaners

Cutting:
Make a pattern for the hands and glove from the pattern graph. Each puppet measures 46 cm (18 in) long. Cut a front glove with sleeve openings and a back without. Cut two sleeves and four felt hands.

86

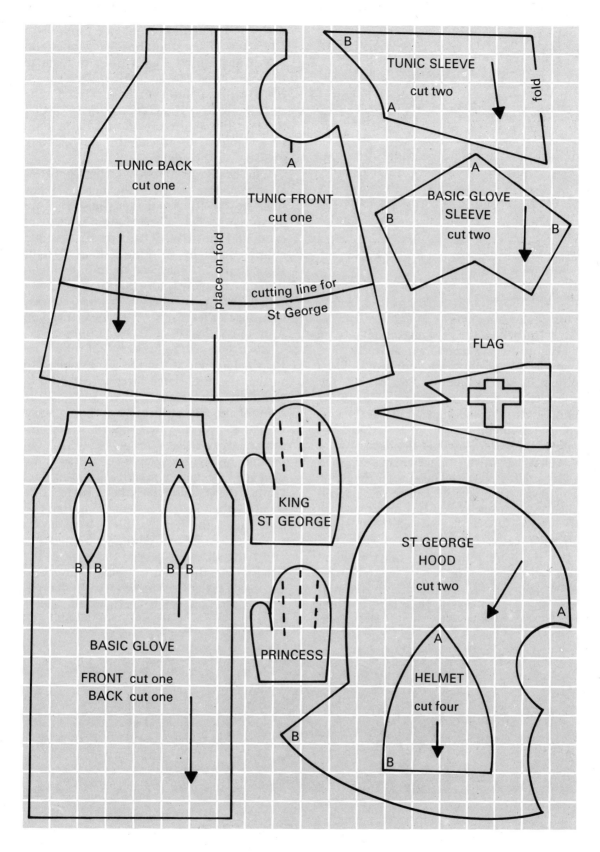

TUNIC SLEEVE
cut two

fold

TUNIC BACK
cut one

TUNIC FRONT
cut one

place on fold

cutting line for
St George

A

B

BASIC GLOVE
SLEEVE
cut two

B

FLAG

A

A

B B B B

BASIC GLOVE

FRONT cut one
BACK cut one

KING
ST GEORGE

PRINCESS

B

ST GEORGE
HOOD

cut two

A

A

HELMET

cut four

B

Pattern graph 24   King, Princess and St George *one square = 2·5 cm (1 in)*

87

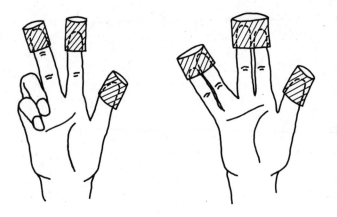

Figure 68 Two suggestions for position of fingers when holding glove puppets

Start by making the card finger stalls. Look at Figure 68 and decide which is the most comfortable position for your hand. Then either make cardboard tubes or cut the toilet roll cylinder to the correct diameter and length. Put the finger stalls to the side for the moment, except for the head stall, and proceed with making the head.

Cut a tube of stocking slightly more than twice the length of the head stall. Push one end down through the centre of the stall then bring it back over the outside and up to the top. Tie both ends of the stocking tightly together with a length of wool. The open end is for your finger while the closed top will be inside the head. Now take up a large handful of stuffing and position it over the top of the stall. Bind it all together

with a long length of wool (see Figure 69). Cut a nose shape from the foam sponge and sew it in position. Cut a band of foam to form the lower jaw and chin. Catch this in place with a few stitches. Stretch the stockinette over the complete head so that the join lies at the crown and back. Fold under any excess stockinette and securely oversew all the edges.

The head will look somewhat shapeless at this stage except for the nose and jaw line. By careful needlemodelling you can create eye sockets, cheeks, mouth, shape of nose and nostrils. The eye sockets are simply made by working a long straight stitch in the correct place and pulling up on it so that a hollow is formed (see Figure 69). Small stitches worked from side to side will raise other parts of the face that you want to emphasize.

Cut a 35·5 cm (14 in) length of tube from the stocking and insert the head in one end so that it comes down level with the neck. Carefully raise that portion covering the front of the face and spread a thin layer of Copydex over the eye sockets, nose and mouth areas. Leave for a little while to become nearly dry then lower the stocking over the face, gently pressing into the glue. Gather the stocking over the crown and tie securely then lower the remaining free end down over the head. Collect both layers under the chin by rolling them together and twist all the excess to the back of the head where they can be secured by hand sewing. This will all be covered by hair.

You are now ready to make the glove.

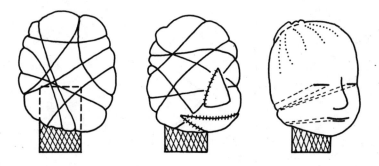

Figure 69 Stages in the making of puppet heads

88

Insert a sleeve into the opening on the front of the glove, matching A to A. Sew on the wrong side of the fabric from B through A to B on the other side. Fold sleeve edges together so that you can sew the underarm seam and opening in glove in one continuous seam. Work second sleeve in the same way. Place front and back gloves right sides together and sew from shoulders down to the hem line. Neaten hem edge. Turn glove right side down and neaten the neck edge. Gather neck and sew to head stall neatly and securely.

Sew felt hands together in pairs. Turn right side out and top stitch finger divisions as indicated on the pattern. Fold a pipe cleaner twice and push into a finger channel. Repeat until all fingers are completed in this way. Now place a little stuffing into the palm of each hand. Cover the finger stalls with stocking as you did for the head stall then push felt wrist over closed end of stall. Insert open end of stall into wrist end of glove sleeve, turn under the raw edge and sew felt to sleeve. You may prefer to glue these fabrics together.

The Princess

Materials: 60 cm (⅔ yd) of 120 cm (48 in) wide fabric makes both glove and tunic
white and blue felt for eyes
2 black, domed buttons for eyes
black embroidery thread for working eyelashes
50 g (2 oz) gold double knitting (thick) wool for hair
30 cm (⅓ yd) of 90 cm (36 in) wide white chiffon for wimple
38 cm (15 in) gold braid for tiara
decorations for tunic (optional)

Cutting: Make a pattern for the tunic from the pattern graph. The back has a diagonal sleeve edge while the tunic front has the large curved sleeve edge. If you cut double sleeves and use one to make a full lining, this will save having a visible wrist edge hem.

Follow the instructions for making both the basic glove and head, modelling a small, feminine nose on the face. Cut white felt eye shapes and blue felt irises, the latter being just slightly larger than the black button pupils. Attach all pieces on to the face in the needlemodelled eye sockets. Work eyelashes in buttonhole stitch along the upper edge of each eye.

Cut the wool for the hair into 80 cm (32 in) lengths and lay these side by side to make a thick band, 10 cm (4 in) wide. Machine a central parting across the band then stitch hair to top of head through the parting. Drape hair over sides and catch at the nape of the neck. Divide each side into three strands and make plaits.

Using Figure 70 as a guide, cut a wimple.

Hem all round the edge then lay over the head, crossing the ends under the chin and tie off at the back of the neck. Make a tiara from the gold braid and place over the wimple so that it covers the front edge. Sew in place to keep it in position.

With right sides together, sew tunic front to back on both sides from neck to upper sleeve edge and from lower sleeve

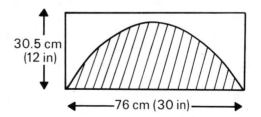

Figure 70 Pattern guide and layout for wimple

edge to hem line. Neaten hem. Make sleeves by folding each in half, right sides together, and matching A to A and B to B. Sew from A to B. Hem the wrist edge. Insert sleeve in sleeve opening of tunic matching A to A and arrange any fullness evenly. Sew sleeve in position. Neaten neck edge and sew tunic to glove neck. Decorate tunic with buttons, braid or lace of your choice, if desired.

The King

Materials:
25 g (1 oz) dish cloth cotton or white double knitting (thick) wool for beard and hair
small pieces of white and green felt for eyes
2 black, domed buttons for eyes
38 cm (15 in) gold braid for crown
jewel for ring (optional)
50 cm (½ yd) of 90 cm (36 in) wide brocade for tunic
1 m (1 yd) of 120 cm (48 in) wide fabric for cloak and cloak lining
chain fastening for cloak

Cutting:
Make the tunic by following the instructions given for the Princess. For the cloak you will need to cut a large circle of fabric having a diameter of 76 cm (30 in). This incorporates a lining and therefore avoids having to make unsightly hems.

Follow the instructions given for making the basic glove and head, modelling a long, masculine nose. Now take a length of dish cloth cotton and cut it into shorter lengths to make the beard. Sew and glue the cotton in place. Sew one group of threads in position on the mouth line. Now with a second group of longer threads, lay these across the mouth and have the ends hanging down on both sides (see Figure 71).

Figure 71 Method of making beard for the King. The upper part of the beard will lie across the lower beard, thus hiding the stitches

Cut the remaining dish cloth cotton into 35·5 cm (14 in) lengths and lay these side by side to make a band 14 cm (5½ in) wide. Machine a central parting across the band then lay the hair over the head and stitch to the puppet through the parting. Glue the rest of the hair to the head on the underside. Brush ends of hair and beard with a suede brush. This will break open the strands and make a fine down, characteristic of an elderly gentleman. Wool can also be used to make the hair and beard, although this is less effective.

Cut eye shapes from white felt and sew these in place with the buttons acting as pupils. Cut eyelids from the green felt and sew these over the upper part of each eye. Finish the head by making a crown from the gold braid.

The hands for this puppet are made from stockinette covered with nylon stocking. Use the pattern for the hand of St George, cutting it slightly larger all round the edge. Fill the hand with stuffing and needlemodel the fingers, sewing a jewel to one finger as a ring, if desired. There is no need to use pipe cleaners in the hands as you can sew the fingers into any position required.

Make the tunic following the instructions given for the Princess. The cloak is very simple to make and could well be used in a shorter version for either the Princess or St George. Following Figure 72 as a guide, fold the cloak in half, right sides together, and cut a 4 cm (1½ in) slit in the centre through both thicknesses. Now sew around the outer curved edge, leaving a 5 cm (2 in) opening and also sew down either side of the slit from the folded edge. Turn cloak right side out and press the edges. Close opening. Lay the cloak over the shoulders with the back of the neck at the base of the slit. Arrange the front edges like lapels and fasten both sides down to the tunic. The back may also need sewing to the puppet if the cloak is heavy. Decorate the front neck of the cloak with a chain fastening.

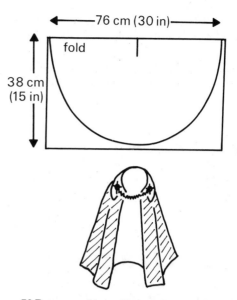

Figure 72 Pattern guide and layout for cloak. Cut this on the fold only if you want cloak and lining combined. Figure also shows finished cloak with chain fastening at the neck

St George

Materials: 50 cm (½ yd) of 90 cm (36 in) wide lurex for basic glove and hood
15 cm (6 in) square of white felt
2 black, domed buttons for eyes
30·5 cm (12 in) square of brown leather cloth or felt
35·5 cm (14 in) silver ribbon for helmet
30 cm (⅓ yd) of 90 cm (36 in) wide linen or calico
76 cm (30 in) red bias binding
48·5 cm (19 in) of 6 mm (¼ in) dowelling rod
red felt for crosses on flag

Cutting: Make a pattern for the helmet and the hood from the pattern graph on page 87. Cut the hood and basic glove from lurex as this represents chain mail. Cut helmet from the leather cloth or felt. The tunic is a shorter, sleeveless version of that worn by the King and Princess and is cut from the linen. The flag is cut from white felt.

Follow instructions for making the basic glove and head, modelling a masculine nose. Cut white felt eye shapes and using the buttons as pupils sew these all in position in the eye sockets. There is no need for hair as the head is covered by the hood. To make the hood, first place both pieces right sides together and sew from A to B, then hem all remaining edges. Turn right side out and lay hood over the head. Catch together at the chin and slip stitch front edges together. You may like to add a chain

fastening under the chin as further decoration.

Sew two helmet pieces together from A to B then repeat with remaining two pieces. Sew both completed halves together. Trim curve and turn the helmet right side out. Check for size. Finish the helmet by gluing the silver ribbon around the lower edge.

Using the shorter back and front tunic pieces, hem each piece separately on all sides. Use red binding to neaten the sleeve and neck edges. You may like to make a small tuck at the neck edge on both sides of the front tunic. This will stop the front gathering up and hiding the cross when the puppet is performing. Make the cross from red binding and hem it in place. The front and back of the tunic are held together by oversewing on each shoulder edge and under each arm. Leave the sides open to allow for greater movement.

Use a piece of sandpaper to both shape and smooth one end of the dowel rod to make a lance. Cut two red felt crosses and stick one to each side of the white felt flag then stick the flag to the shaped end of the lance. Look at the illustration facing page 80 to work out a suitable position. Place the lance in the hand and bend the fingers around to grip it. The lance can be placed under one arm when St George charges the dragon. This will have to be done off stage. Use the lance as Punch would use his stick, bashing, hitting and poking at the dragon. A good fight is a very necessary end to your puppet play.

The Dragon

Materials: 38 cm (15 in) square of red felt
33 × 17·5 cm (13 × 7 in) rust felt
50 cm (½ yd) of 120 cm (48 in) wide red fabric
38 cm (15 in) square of white felt
170 g (6 oz) stuffing
23 cm (9 in) square of stiff card
23 cm (9 in) square of scrap material
1 m (1 yd) gold cord for mouth edging
30·5 × 15 cm (12 × 6 in) gold felt for tongue
28 cm (11 in) wire for tongue
small pieces of black and yellow felt for eyes

Cutting: Make a set of patterns from the pattern graph. The finished dragon measures 51 cm (20 in) long. Cut head, eyebrows, lower jaw and ears from red fabric. Cut a sleeve from the same fabric measuring 35·5 cm (14 in) by 40·5 cm (16 in) long. From the red felt cut mouth linings, the crested back ridge and approximately fifty scales. Cut two scalloped back ridges from rust felt and approximately sixteen scales. Cut teeth from white felt and two 7·5 cm (3 in) diameter circles for the eyes. Cut tongue from gold felt.

Start by making the sleeve of the puppet. Sandwich a red felt crest between two rust scalloped crests and then lay all three on the long edge of the sleeve, fold over opposite long edge and sew the centre back seam on the wrong side. Place the crest 2·5 cm (1 in) back from what will become the front of the sleeve. Make a hem on the opposite edge of the sleeve. Turn right side out and put the sleeve aside for the moment and concentrate on making the head. Figure 73 shows how the head and sleeve pieces are arranged and how the hand fits in the puppet.

Make the upper and lower sets of teeth next. Place a pair of felt pieces together and sew along the jagged edge. Cut off points and clip into the corners before turning right side out. Stuff the point of each tooth then baste the open edges together. Hold stuffing away from the base of the teeth with pins or large tacking stitches. Make remaining three sets of teeth in the same way.

Now prepare the lower jaws so that the teeth may be sewn in place. Ease the lower jaw around the curved edge until it fits the felt mouth lining. Insert the two lower sets of teeth, arranging them evenly on either side of the jaw, and then sew all together on the wrong side leaving the straight edge open. Turn jaw right side out and remove pins from base of teeth. Cut a card stiffener to fit in the jaw against the felt lining. Then make a pattern for the thumb stall from the guide line marked on the mouth lining

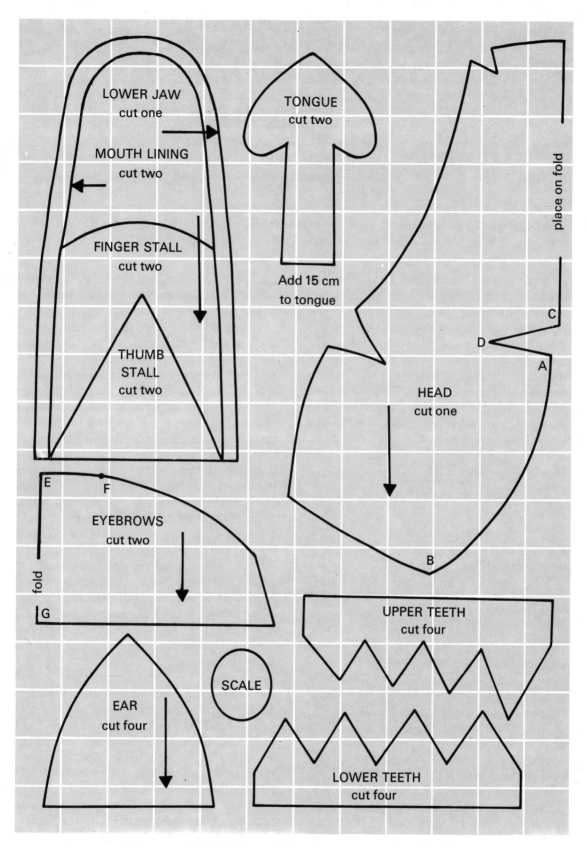

LOWER JAW
cut one

MOUTH LINING
cut two

FINGER STALL
cut two

THUMB
STALL
cut two

TONGUE
cut two

Add 15 cm
to tongue

place on fold

HEAD
cut one

C

D

A

B

E

F

EYEBROWS
cut two

fold

G

SCALE

UPPER TEETH
cut four

EAR
cut four

LOWER TEETH
cut four

Pattern graph 25   St George's Dragon *one square = 2·5 cm (1 in)*

93

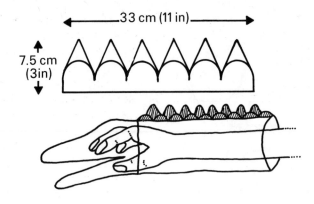

Figure 73 Suggested guide for cutting the sleeve crest. Also, outline drawing of the Dragon to show sleeve tube, head and position of hand and arm needed to operate the puppet

pattern. Cut two from scrap fabric and sew together round the curved edge. Push stuffing into the front end of the jaw between the card and the fabric then insert the thumb stall until all straight edges are level. Turn under raw edges and hem so that the opening is only into the thumb stall (see Figure 74). Lay half the gold cord around the edge of the mouth and catch in place with invisible stitching. The lower jaw is now finished.

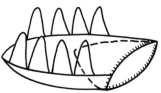

Figure 74 Lower jaw of Dragon showing pocket that acts as a stall for the thumb

Fold the head in half with right sides facing. Match A to A and B to B then sew the seam from A to B. Now match As to C and sew seam from D through C to D on the other side. There are two darts to sew on each side of the head; they are the small nostril dart and the larger cheek dart. Now insert mouth lining and both sets of upper teeth. Use the nostril darts as markers for placing them evenly on either side of the upper jaw. Sew from one side of the jaw round to the other. Turn head right side out, remove pins and make card stiffener and finger stall as you did for the lower jaw. Stuff the front of the head and the crown firmly but leave enough space to insert the finger stall through the opening so that it lies just above the card stiffener. Turn under

all raw edges and hem finger stall to head fabric gathering the latter where necessary to get a good fit.

Sew gold cord to edge of mouth as you did for the lower jaw. Sew both felt tongue pieces together around the outside edge and form a channel for the wire by following Figure 75. Now bind both ends of the wire then thread it into the channel from the throat end. Sew this same end to the back edge of the upper mouth. It will hang down better from here in the finished puppet. It can also be bent into any required shape, curling out amongst the teeth.

Gather the outside edge of each white felt eye circle to make stuffed eyes. Insert a knobble of stuffing in each before you pull up and fasten off the gathering thread. Sew eyeballs to each side of the head then cut yellow irises and black pupils from felt and hem a set to each eyeball. Place both eyebrow fabric pieces right sides together and sew around the outside edge leaving open between E and F. Turn right side out and close the opening. Lay eyebrows over both eyes so that G lies between the eyes and on the top of the head in a central position. Ladder stitch eyebrows down to each side of the head by working from G, over the eyes and around the back towards either E or F. There will be a ridge of excess material between E and F which can be pressed together to form a crest on top of the head. Look at the colour illustrations to see how all the pieces are related.

Sew ears together in pairs on the wrong side, leaving the base open. Turn right side

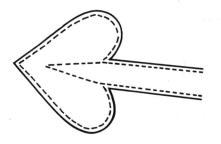

Figure 75 Dragon's tongue, showing lines of top stitching to be worked either by hand or machine

out and close the opening, pulling up on the thread so that each ear becomes 'cupped'. Position the ears on the back edge of the eyebrow shield and ladder stitch them in place. The head is now completed and ready to join to the sleeves but first catch upper and lower mouths together along the straight edge by the throat. A clever toymaker might like to leave this open so that St George's lance could slide straight down the gullet of the Dragon. Turn under the raw edge on the front of the sleeve then ladder stitch it to the back of the head, leaving the openings to the finger and thumb stalls clear. Catch just enough head to make a secure join otherwise you will not be able to operate the mouth so effectively.

Glue scales over the back of the head and use them to conceal the join between the head and sleeve. Continue gluing them down the sides of the body, interspersing a few rust-coloured scales amongst the mass of red ones. A patterned fabric would require fewer scales. Decide how much finishing your own dragon requires.

13　The Dragon

Ancient folklore is rich in legends of both fearsome and lovable dragons. So popular are they that present-day writers still try to capture the magic of dragonland for children in modern stories. The toy given here is a lovable young dragon – a suitable friend for any child.

Materials:
1·2 m (1⅓ yd) of 120 cm (48 in) wide red fabric
25 cm (¼ yd) of contrasting fabric for wings and mouth lining
23 cm (9 in) square of yellow felt
17·5 cm (7 in) wire for tongue
30·5 × 61 cm (12 × 24 in) foam sheeting, 12 mm (½ in) thick
1·6 kg (3 lb 8 oz) stuffing
30·5 cm (12 in) square gold felt
8 pipe cleaners
1 m (1 yd) gold braid
15 cm (6 in) square of white felt
2 flat buttons, 4 cm (1½ in) in diameter
small piece of black felt

Cutting:
Make a set of patterns from the pattern graph. The pattern for the tongue is taken from St George's dragon, making a total of fifteen pieces of pattern to work from. When finished, Dragon stands 46 cm (18 in) high and is 68·5 cm (27 in) to the tip of his tail. Cut a pair of wings and the mouth linings from the contrasting fabric. The fingers and claws are cut from gold felt, the tongue from yellow felt. All remaining pieces are cut from the main fabric and are as follows: a pair each of head, body, tail, wing, sole and upper feet pieces, two pairs each of arms, ears and legs and one only head gusset, body gusset and lower jaw.

Start by making the body, because all other parts of the toy are added to it as they are completed. Place a tail to the body, right sides together and A and B matching, sew. Repeat on the other side. Now insert body gusset between both bodies, matching C to C on each side of the neck and D to D. Sew gusset in place. Sew the centre back seam from E, around the tail and back along to D on the underside, remembering to leave the small opening in the tail. Sew this seam twice, then trim the curves.

Insert head gusset between both head pieces, matching F to F on each side and G to G, sew on the wrong side. Attach a mouth lining, matching I to I on each side and sew, leaving the straight edge open. Sew the second mouth lining to the lower jaw, again matching I to I, then position lower jaw in base of head matching H to H and I to I on each side. Sew in place and also make the dart in the lower jaw.

Make the tongue, following the instructions given for St George's dragon, remembering that it will not have to be as long. When made, position it centrally between the linings at the back of the mouth and sew securely in place. The head may now be turned right side out and pushed through the neck opening of the body. G will be at the centre back while the dart in the lower jaw will mark the centre front spot. Take care not to trap the tongue. Now sew round the neck join several times.

The completed skin may now be turned right side out, ready for stuffing. Cut a

Local Dragons (*opposite*)
Left : Suffolk Wyvern. *Middle :* Laidly Worm. *Right :* Nessie.

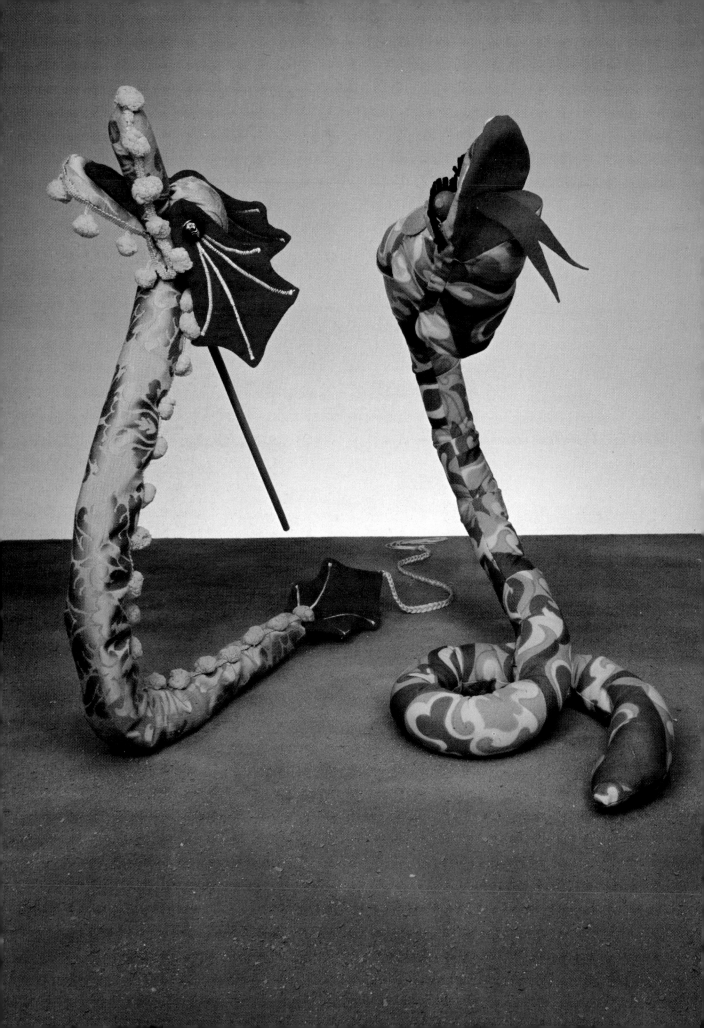

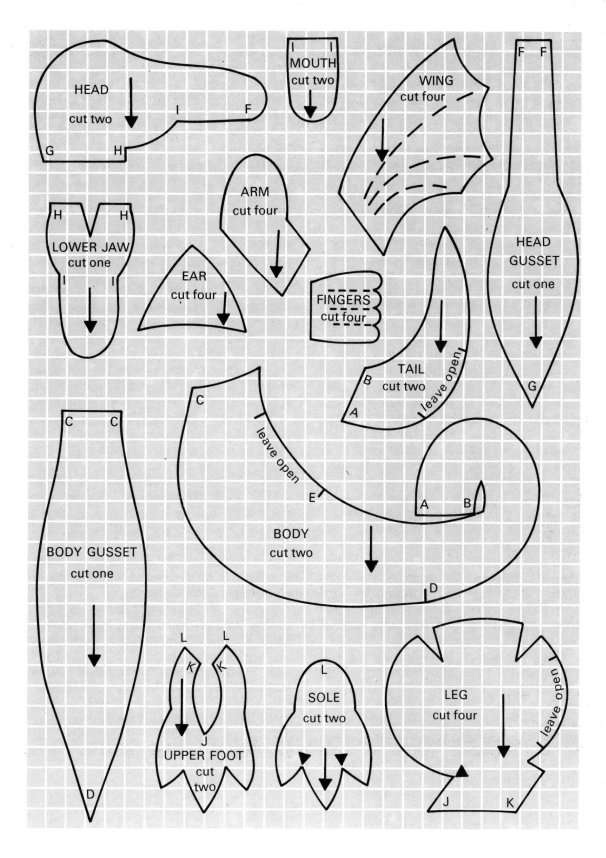

Pattern graph 26   Dragon *one square = 2·5 cm (1 in)*

Serpents (*opposite*)
Left : Carnival Rod Dragon. *Right :* Snake Glove Puppet.

foam shape to fit in the lower jaw. The remainder of the body is stuffed through the back opening and through the underside of the tail. When the dragon feels really firm, close both openings with ladder stitch.

Place right sides of the fabric wing piece and a contrasting coloured lining together. Sew around the outer edge, trim curves and then turn right side out. Cut a piece of foam to fit into the wing then turn under raw edges and close the opening. Now top stitch four veins on the wing following the guide lines marked on the pattern. If you have a zig zag foot on your machine then use this to do the top stitching, using a contrasting coloured thread to highlight the veins. Make the second wing in the same way, then hand sew them together at the base so that the linings face outwards. Position the paired wings on the centre back seam and ladder stitch them in place.

Take up a pair of leg pieces and sew the two darts on the upper curve of both sides then place them right sides together and sew from J around the curve to the opening on the back edge. Sew upper foot to leg, matching J to J and K to K on each side. Now close back leg seam from L through K and up to the opening on the back edge. Insert sole, matching L to L and sew all round the edge. Trim curves, clip between toes and turn completed leg right side out. Stuff foot and ankle firmly, and the large bulbous hip less so. Make second leg in the same way then position them on the body so that the dragon stands balanced. The hips will lie higher than the centre back seam giving the dragon an appearance of being at rest. Ladder stitch legs to body.

Trace the outline of each toe from the pattern and use this to cut felt claws. Cut the claws about 2 mm larger on all sides and also cut them in pairs so that you have twelve claws, making six pairs. Top stitch each pair on the outer edge then push them over a toe and hem in place.

Place a felt hand to the end of each arm piece and sew the two together across the wrist. The width of the felt hand is purposely less than that of the arm, so don't stretch the felt to make it fit. Assemble the arms in pairs, sewing round the curved edge of the fabric only and leaving an opening for turning. Turn arm right side out and top stitch the hand. Work stitching down either side of each guide line marked on the pattern. Do this carefully and you will be able to slash between the four fingers. Fold a pipe cleaner in half then push it into a finger channel. Repeat for the remaining three fingers then stuff any gaps, the hands and lastly the arm. Close the opening and ladder stitch the arm to the body. Work the second arm in exactly the same way. The fingers can of course be bent into a variety of positions.

It only remains now to finish the head and the dragon comes alive. Sew the braid around the edge of the mouth, extending it at the corners so that it gives the appearance of lengthening the mouth. Cut two small circles of gold felt and either glue or hem them in place as nostrils. Make the eyes from two 9 cm ($3\frac{1}{2}$ in) diameter circles of white felt. Gather the edge of the circle and slightly pull up on the thread, insert a knobble of stuffing and then one of the flat buttons. Finish gathering up the felt and fasten off. Ladder stitch the eyeball to the side of the head. Cut a circle of black felt and hem it to the eye as a pupil. Make second eye in the same way.

Finally, sew the ears together in pairs, leaving the base open. Turn right side out and cut a foam shape to act as both filling and stiffener for the ear. Insert the foam and close the opening. Pull up on the closing stitches so that the ear becomes cup-shaped. When both ears are completed, arrange them on the head to find the best position, then ladder stitch them securely in place. Your dragon is now ready to play with.

14 Local Dragons

The British Isles have a folklore that is rich in regional dragons, monsters and serpents. There are the more well known dragons of Wales and Ulster, tales of knights like Sir Tristam and Sir Launcelot slaying dragons, legends of battles among Celtic tribes who referred to the enemy chief as a dragon; while many local woods and castles have dragons closely associated with them.

Suffolk Wyvern

Wyverns are heraldic winged dragons differing from all other dragons by having only two legs. The body of this toy is made from unstuffed, gathered circles of fabric which are known as Suffolk Puffs. These puffs are collected together and threaded on to elastic, which gives the Wyvern a mobility that is quite uncharacteristic of conventionally stuffed soft toys.

Materials:
- 2 m (2¼ yd) of 120 cm (48 in) wide fabric
- 2 m (2¼ yd) millinery elastic
- 4 raincoat buttons to act as elastic stops
- 30·5 (12 in) square of foam sheeting, 12 mm (½ in) thick
- 15 cm (6 in) square of yellow felt
- 84 g (3 oz) stuffing for head
- 2 buttons for eyes

Cutting: Prepare patterns for head, ears, wings and tail from the pattern graph. You will also need circle templates cut from card, with diameters of 20 cm (8 in), 17·5 cm (7 in), 15 cm (6 in), 12·5 cm (5 in) and 10 cm (4 in) respectively. This makes a Wyvern approximately 66 cm (26 in) long. Cut all pattern pieces from fabric and the body circles as follows:

12 circles 20 cm (8 in) in diameter
14 circles 17·5 cm (7 in) in diameter
10 circles 15 cm (6 in) in diameter
12 circles 12·5 cm (5 in) in diameter
22 circles 10 cm (4 in) in diameter
Figure 76 shows how these circles are to be arranged. Reserve two 20 cm (8 in) circles to make the feet.

Figure 76 Suffolk Wyvern, showing how the fabric circles are to be arranged

99

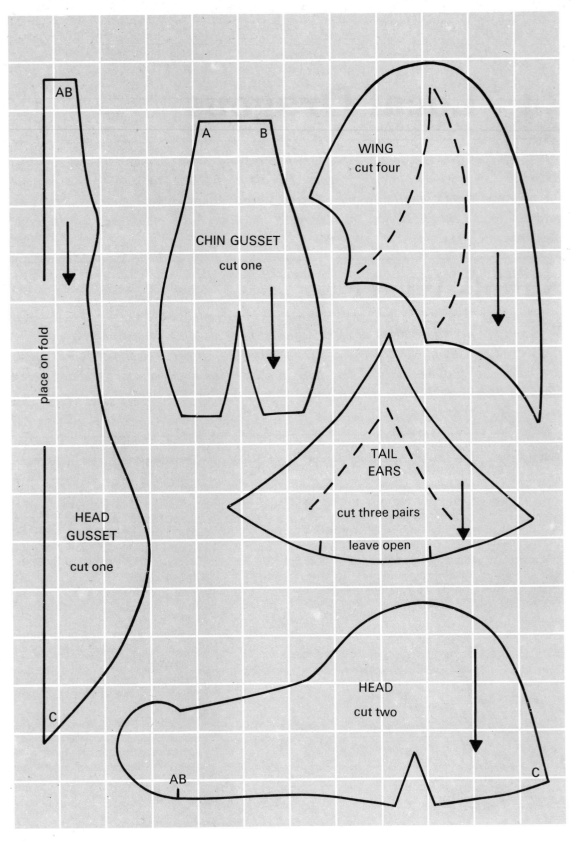

Pattern graph 27   Suffolk Wyvern *one square = 2·5 cm (1 in)*

100

Start by preparing the fabric circles for the body as this is a long process. Run a gathering thread around the edge of each circle, pull up and fasten off. Flatten the circles between your fingers to make discs then pierce the centre of each disc so that you make a hole opposite the gathers. Elastic will be threaded through the holes to hold all the discs together.

Cut a 127 cm (50 in) length of elastic and thread a button on to it. Position the button exactly half way along the elastic and knot it in place. Now thread the two ends through a bodkin and start forming the body. Work from the shoulders back towards the tail so that the first discs to be threaded on are the largest followed by the smaller sizes. Finish off the end by tying a button on to the elastic. Leave just sufficient slack in the elastic so that the body may be pulled like a spring.

Place right sides of both tail pieces together and sew around the outside. Turn right side out and cut a foam shape to fit inside the tail. Top stitch along the guide line marked on the pattern. Position the opening of the tail over the button at the end of the body and then sew the last body circle to the tail so that the button is enclosed.

Make the wings by sewing each fabric pair of pieces together on the wrong side. Turn right side out and cut foam shapes to fit inside each wing. Make the veins by top stitching along the guide lines marked on the pattern. Do this in a contrasting coloured thread for greater effect. Close base of wings then sew them on to the top of the tenth shoulder disc.

Cut the remaining piece of elastic into a 46 cm (18 in) length and tie a button in the centre as you did for the body elastic. Thread on seven discs for one leg then pass the bodkin between the body elastic of the ninth and tenth shoulder discs. Thread on seven more discs to make the second leg and tie off the ends on the last button. Each foot is made from a 20 cm (8 in) fabric circle. Gather the circle and flatten into a disc. Do not pierce a hole, instead, fold the edges in towards the centre so that you form a triangle (see Figure 77). Fasten the button from the base of the leg to the foot, just under the three folds. Now stitch foot to the last leg disc so that the button is both securely held and out of sight. Sew felt claws together in pairs then push one over each point of the foot and catch in place. Make both feet in the same way so that they each have three claws.

Sew chin gusset to head gusset on the wrong side, matching A to A and B to B. Sew cheek darts on each side of the head then insert completed gusset between sides, matching C to C, and sew. Turn the head right side out and stuff firmly through the opening in the chin gusset. Close opening and at the last moment push the shoulder button into the head and fasten it securely in place as you finish closing the head.

Make the ears by sewing each pair on the wrong side. Turn right side out and gather up the opening as you close it. Position ears on the head and sew in place. Sew buttons on as eyes or cut felt shapes and sew these in place if the toy is for a very young child.

Once you understand the technique behind making the Wyvern you should be able to make a more conventional dragon by simply adding another pair of legs. The Suffolk Puffs could also be made from all your leftover pieces of dressweight material, making a gloriously multicoloured monster for very little cost.

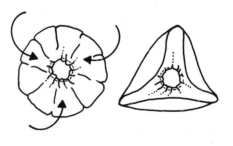

Figure 77 Construction of foot for Suffolk Wyvern, showing gathered circle and how the three sides are folded in to form the toes

Nessie

Traditionally many Scottish lochs are thought to be inhabited by mysterious animals, perhaps even plesiosaurs, although recently attention has centred on the famous or infamous Loch Ness monster.

Materials:
50 cm (½ yd) of 120 cm (48 in) wide fabric
23 cm (9 in) square of foam sheeting, 12 mm (½ in) thick
250 ml (½ pint) Polybeads or 454 g (1 lb) foam chips
15 cm (6 in) square of white felt for eyes
84 g (3 oz) stuffing for head
7·5 cm (3 in) square of black felt for eyes
38 cm (15 in) square of felt for fins
4 buttons to decorate fins

Cutting:
For the head use the pattern of the Suffolk Wyvern, omitting the ears, and cut eyelids from the pattern for the Snake glove puppet. Cut four pairs of felt fins, using the pattern graph to make a pattern. Cut the body tube from Figure 78: as this is a very simple shape you should be able to cut it free hand. When finished, Nessie is approximately 122 cm (48 in) long.

Open out the fabric to full width and cut the head gusset as close to the selvage as possible, then fold the fabric in half widthways so that you have a double thickness approximately 112 cm (44 in) wide. Cut the body tube first, then the remaining pieces of the head. Working on the wrong side of the fabric, sew round the outside leaving the neck end open. Turn right side out and cut foam shapes to insert in the tail lobes. Now top stitch the end of the tube into a point so that it separates the tail from the tube proper. Loosely fill the tube with Polybeads or foam chips, leaving sufficient slack so that Nessie may be coiled easily. Cut a circle of foam to fit in the neck and then turn under the raw edges and sew the neck to the foam collar. Make the head from instructions given for the Wyvern, then ladder stitch it to the tube.

Cut two 6·5 cm (2½ in) diameter circles of white felt and make these into eyeballs by gathering up the edges and inserting a knobble of stuffing before finishing off the gathering thread. Cut black pupils and glue these in place, then sew completed eyeballs to the side of the head. Use the eyelid of the Snake, on page 107. You will only need a single thickness of eyelid as it can be sewn closely round the eyeball. Add eyelashes if you want a more friendly monster.

Make the fins by top stitching each felt pair together, preferably using a coloured thread for contrast. The fins may then be stitched permanently on to the side of the body and the buttons attached. You may prefer to make buttonholes in the fins and sew the buttons to the tube so that a child can practise putting on and taking off the fins.

Being such a simple pattern, it is very easy to adapt Nessie into other monsters, serpents or snakes. The Laidly Worm which follows is an example.

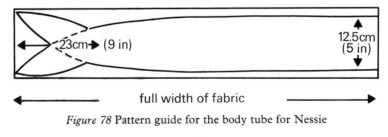

Figure 78 Pattern guide for the body tube for Nessie

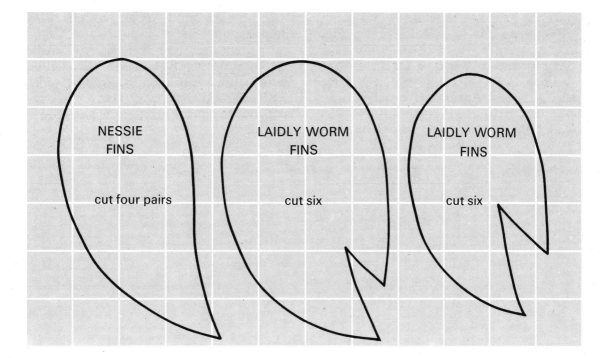

Pattern graph 28   Nessie and Laidly Worm *one square = 2·5 cm (1 in)*

The Laidly Worm

There lived a long time ago in Bamborough Castle, which is in Northern England, a very beautiful princess. Yet in true fairy book tradition she had a jealous stepmother who changed her into a dreadful worm-like dragon. Fortunately a brother, returning from abroad, rescued her from this horrible fate and in turn the stepmother became an ugly toad.

Materials: 50 cm (½ yd) of 120 cm (48 in) wide fabric
stuffing and foam as for Nessie
2 30·5 cm (12 in) squares of different coloured felts
4 buttons for fins
2 knobbly gold buttons for eyes

Cutting: Use the patterns for Nessie to make the head and body. Make a pattern for the fins from the pattern graph. Cut six fins from each square of felt, one set being slightly larger than the other so that the edge of each fin when finished appears coloured. The Worm is approximately 122 cm (48 in) long.

Make the head and body for the Worm.

Place a large and a small felt fin together and top stitch them with contrasting coloured thread. Work all six fins in this way but make sure that you have three pairs at the end. Again, like Nessie, button-holes may be worked on the fins. Position two of the fins on each side of the tail lobes and sew on the buttons to hold them in place.

The remaining pair of fins is used to make eye backings for the knobbly button eyes. Look at the illustration facing page 96 to see how they are arranged. Because of their size and shape they make the Worm appear very fierce.

15 Serpents

Serpents are usually regarded as scaly limbless reptiles, and while this certainly describes all the snakes it also includes many dragons and sea monsters. The Chinese for instance, believe that dragons hatch from an egg as a serpent and then take some 2000 years to grow into full-fledged dragons complete with horns and wings. Both the toys in this chapter have been made as rather unusual puppets.

Snake Glove Puppet

Although the snake has been made with a conventional sleeve to wear on the arm it also has a long coiling body tube. It is this tube that provides all the fun for it enables the snake to be coiled either around the sleeve or around the neck and body of the child operating the puppet.

Materials:
    1 m (1 yd) of 120 cm (48 in) wide fabric
    23 cm (9 in) square of felt
    strip of red felt for tongue
    566 g (1 lb 4 oz) stuffing
    15 cm (6 in) square of felt for scales
    2 large beads for eyes
    7.5 cm (3 in) square of black felt

Cutting:
    Make a set of patterns from the pattern graph. This makes a puppet about 2 m (2 yd) long. Open out the fabric and refold according to Figure 79. This allows you to cut two 20 cm (8 in) wide bias strips for the body tube as well as all the other fabric parts. Cut mouth lining from the large square of felt.

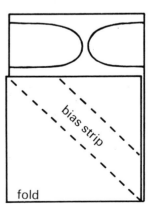

Figure 79 Fabric layout for Snake Glove Puppet, showing how two bias strips can be cut

Working on the wrong side of the fabric sew upper and lower sleeves together down each side from X to the arm opening. Insert mouth lining matching upper and lower jaws and X to X on each side. Sew in place. Hem arm opening and turn sleeve right side out. Glue tongue in place on the roof of the mouth.

To make the body tube, sew the two bias strips together then fold the strip in half, lengthways and sew it into a tube by following Figure 80. This shows the tail shaping. Shape the head end by cutting off the single thickness of fabric. Sew short back seam of collar by bringing B to B then

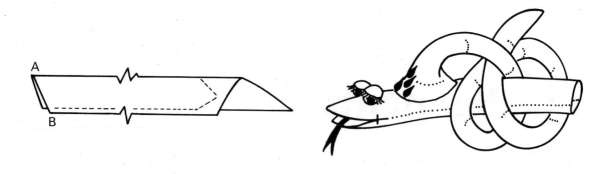

Figure 80 Construction of tube for Snake Glove Puppet, and line drawing showing relationship of the tube to the sleeve of the puppet

insert head end of body tube matching A to A and B to B, and sew. The coiling of the tube is achieved by sewing twelve curved darts across the seam, each 12·5 cm (5 in) apart (see Figure 81). Turn tube right side out and stuff fairly firmly, then turn under raw edges of the collar and ladder stitch it to the upper sleeve, inserting any more additional stuffing that may be needed. You will find it easier to do this if you put a rolled newspaper inside the sleeve. Cover the seams on the front of the collar with a few felt scales glued in place.

To make the eyes, first sew the small shaping dart in each eyelid then place a pair right sides together with a felt eyelash strip laid along the straight edge. Sew round the edge, leaving a small opening. Turn right side out and loosely stuff the eyelid. Fringe the eyelash. Sew beads in place as eyes and stick small black pupils on them, then ladder stitch each eyelid over an eye.

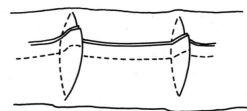

Figure 81 Body tube for Snake Glove Puppet, showing two of the curved, shaping darts worked across the seam

106

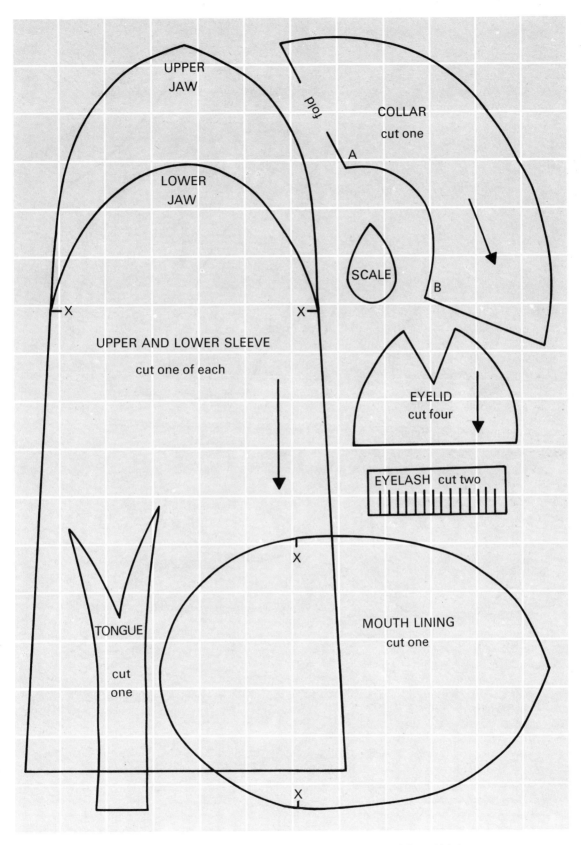

UPPER JAW

LOWER JAW

COLLAR
cut one

fold

A

SCALE

B

UPPER AND LOWER SLEEVE

cut one of each

EYELID
cut four

EYELASH cut two

TONGUE

cut one

MOUTH LINING
cut one

X

X

X

X

X

Pattern graph 29   Snake Glove Puppet *one square = 2·5 cm (1 in)*

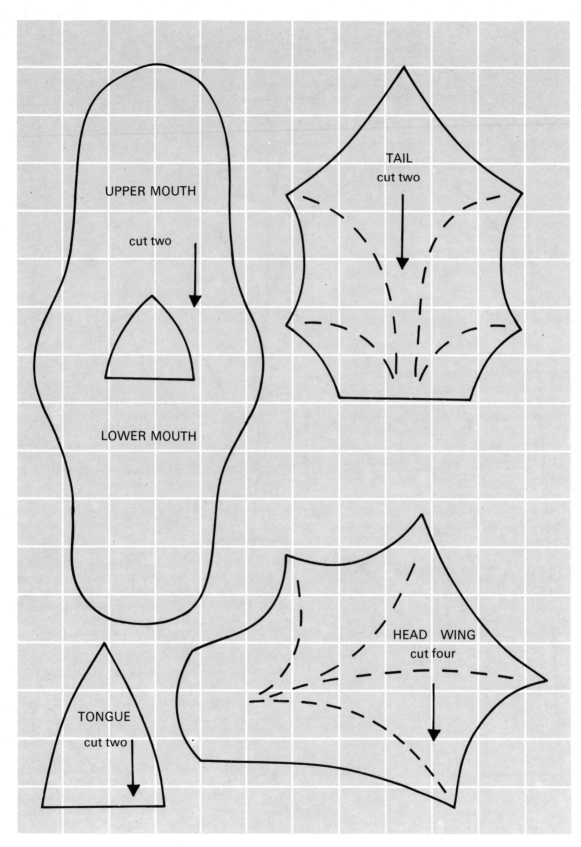

UPPER MOUTH

cut two

LOWER MOUTH

TAIL
cut two

HEAD WING
cut four

TONGUE
cut two

Pattern graph 30   Carnival Rod Dragon *one square = 2·5 cm (1 in)*

108

Carnival Rod Dragon

In the Far East, serpents and dragons are both symbols of authority and traditional festival animals, often being exotically coloured and very fanciful. This is not surprising when you realize that Chinese dragons had nine resemblances, namely the horns of a deer, head of a camel, eyes of a devil, neck of a snake, abdomen of a large cockle, scales of a carp, claws of an eagle, soles of a tiger and the ears of an ox. The Carnival Rod Dragon is a smaller version of those found in many street festivals, which often require three or more people to work them.

Materials:
- 1 m (1 yd) of dowelling rod, 10 mm (⅜ in) in diameter
- 50 cm (½ yd) of 120 cm (48 in) wide fabric
- 25 cm (¼ yd) of 120 cm (48 in) wide red satin
- 40·5 cm (16 in) square of foam sheeting, 12 mm (½ in) thick
- 2 m (2¼ yd) bobble fringe
- 56 g (2 oz) stuffing for head
- 2 buttons for eyes
- 2 small eyes and 1 hook from hook and eye units
- 86 cm (34 in) curtain wire
- 16 table tennis balls
- gold cord for hand control at end of tail

Cutting:
Make a set of patterns from the pattern graph. This makes a rod puppet 1 m (1 yd) long. Cut a body tube from the fabric measuring 16·5 cm (6½ in) deep by 76 cm (30 in) wide. You will need a card template 17·5 cm (7 in) in diameter for cutting the head circle. Cut head circle and mouth from fabric and tail, head wings and tongue from red satin. Cut foam shapes to fit tail, mouth and head wings then cut the rest of the foam into sixteen 2·5 cm (1 in) squares.

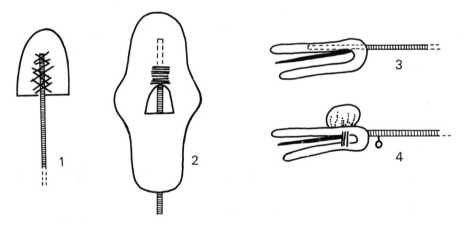

Figure 82 Stages in the construction of the head for Carnival Rod Dragon
1 Foam shape stitched to rod 2 Rod and foam inserted in the upper mouth 3 Tongue stitched to roof of mouth 4 Upper and lower mouth stitched together on the bend and head shape ladder stitched to back of upper mouth

Start by making the head. Use a scrap of foam to protect the head end of the rod. Hold it in place and oversew securely to the rod (see Figure 82). Now sew both mouth pieces together around the outside edge and on the wrong side. Turn right side out through central opening and insert a foam shaped filling. Push protected end of rod into upper mouth and securely catch it in place by oversewing from top of mouth through to inside roof of mouth. Sew both pieces of tongue together on the wrong side, leaving the base open. Turn right side out and insert foam shaping. Close opening and sew the tongue to the back of the roof of the mouth. Turn under the raw edges of the central mouth opening and slip stitch the edges together. Fold lower mouth forward and oversew on each side to hold in place (see Figure 82). Sew bobble fringe around the edge of the mouth.

Now gather the head circle but before closing off, insert a knobble of stuffing. Position head on the back of the upper mouth where the rod emerges and ladder stitch both together and as neatly as possible, even pulling the head down on either side of the rod if necessary. Sew pairs of head wings together on the wrong side. Turn right side out and insert foam shaping. Close the opening and top stitch the veins with coloured thread. Sew a wing to each side of the head and catch in place by sewing on the button eyes.

Screw an eye into one end of the curtain wire then thread on from the other end a ball, then a square of foam then another ball and so on until all the balls and foam squares are in place along the wire. Trim foam squares into rounds. Fold the fabric body tube in half widthways and then sew the long seam on the wrong side. Turn tube right side out and then feed in the wire and ball skeleton. Gather up and fasten off the end with the eye in it.

Make the tail by sewing both pieces together on the wrong side. Turn right side out and insert foam filling. Top stitch veins with coloured thread then push end of curtain wire through the centre of the tail. Stitch tail to the end of the body tube and finally insert an eye in the end of the curtain wire. It may be necessary to cut the wire shorter as the eye should be at the end of the tail. Tie a cord on to the tail eye. Finish by sewing bobble fringe along the crest.

Finally, screw a hook into the rod at the neck and then hook on the body. Hold the rod in your left hand and move the dragon by controlling the cord in your right hand. The rod may need to be cut shorter if the dragon is heavy and therefore unbalanced. Smooth the cut end with fine grade sandpaper.

INDEX